Responsive Web Design
by Example Beginner's Guide

Second Edition

Build powerful and engaging responsive websites with ease

Thoriq Firdaus

[PACKT] open source✲
PUBLISHING   community experience distilled

BIRMINGHAM - MUMBAI

Responsive Web Design by Example Beginner's Guide
Second Edition

First published: March 2013

Second edition: November 2014

Production reference: 1171114

Published by Packt Publishing Ltd.
Livery Place
35 Livery Street
Birmingham B3 2PB, UK.

ISBN 978-1-78355-325-9

www.packtpub.com

Credits

Author

Thoriq Firdaus

Reviewers

Saumya Dwivedi

Gabriel Hilal

Joydip Kanjilal

Anirudh Prabhu

Taroon Tyagi

Commissioning Editor

Julian Ursell

Acquisition Editor

Sam Wood

Content Development Editor

Kirti Patil

Technical Editor

Anand Singh

Copy Editors

Sarang Chari

Shambhavi Pai

Project Coordinator

Kranti Berde

Proofreaders

Maria Gould

Lesley Harrison

Linda Morris

Indexers

Rekha Nair

Priya Sane

Production Coordinator

Kyle Albuquerque

Cover Work

Kyle Albuquerque

About the Author

Thoriq Firdaus is a web developer and lives in Indonesia. He has been dabbling in web design and development for more than 5 years, working with many clients of varying sizes. He appreciates the giving nature of the web design community at large. He also loves trying out new things in CSS3 and HTML5 and occasionally speaks at some local colleges and institutions on the subject.

Outside of work, he loves spending time with his wife and daughter, watching movies, and enjoying meals at nearby cafes and restaurants.

About the Reviewers

Saumya Dwivedi is currently a member of the technical staff of Groupon India Pvt. Ltd. She obtained a BTech degree in Computer Science from the International Institute of Information Technology, Hyderabad. She is a software enthusiast and worked on the responsive design of Gnome websites during one of her internships. She hails from Indore (Madhya Pradesh) and currently resides in Chennai.

Gabriel Hilal is a full-stack web developer specializing in Ruby on Rails and related technologies. He has a Bachelor's degree in Information Systems (Internet Business) and a Master's degree in Information Systems with Management Studies, both from Kingston University, London. During his time at the university, he developed a passion for Ruby on Rails, and since then, he has done freelance work using behavior-driven development and agile methodologies to build high-quality Rails applications. He can be contacted via his website (www.gabrielhilal.com) or by e-mail at gabriel@gabrielhilal.com.

Joydip Kanjilal is a Microsoft Most Valuable Professional in ASP.NET, speaker, and author of several books and articles. He has more than 16 years of experience in IT, with more than 10 years in Microsoft .NET and related technologies. He has been selected as MSDN Featured Developer of the Fortnight (MSDN) a number of times and also as Community Credit Winner at www.community-credit.com several times.

He is the author of the following books:

- *Visual Studio 2010 and .NET 4 Six in One, Wiley India Private Limited*
- *ASP.NET 4.0 Programming, McGraw-Hill Osborne*
- *Entity Framework Tutorial, Packt Publishing*
- *Pro Sync Framework, Apress*
- *Sams Teach Yourself ASP.NET Ajax in 24 Hours, Sams*
- *ASP.NET Data Presentation Controls Essentials, Packt Publishing*

He is the reviewer of the following books:

- *jQuery UI Cookbook, Packt Publishing*
- *Instant Testing with QUnit, Packt Publishing*
- *Instant jQuery Selectors, Packt Publishing*
- *C# 5 First Look, Packt Publishing*
- *jQuery 1.3 Reference Guide, Packt Publishing*
- *HTML 5 Step by Step, O'Reilly Media*

He has authored more than 250 articles for some of the most reputable sites, such as www.msdn.microsoft.com, www.code-magazine.com, www.asptoday.com, www.devx.com, www.ddj.com, www.aspalliance.com, www.aspnetpro.com, www.sql-server-performance.com, www.sswug.org, and so on. A lot of these articles have been selected and published on www.asp.net—Microsoft's official site on ASP.NET.

He has years of experience in designing and architecting solutions for various domains. His technical strengths include C, C++, VC++, Java, C# 5, Microsoft .NET, Ajax, WCF 4, ASP.NET MVC 4, ASP.NET Web API, REST, SOA, design patterns, SQL Server 2012, Google's Protocol Buffers, WPF, Silverlight 5, operating systems, and computer architecture.

He blogs at http://aspadvice.com/blogs/joydip and his website is www.joydipkanjilal.com. You can follow him on Twitter at https://twitter.com/joydipkanjilal and on Facebook at https://www.facebook.com/joydipkanjilal. You can also find him on LinkedIn at http://in.linkedin.com/in/joydipkanjilal.

I would like to thank my family for providing me with the support to make this book a success.

Anirudh Prabhu is a software engineer (Web) with more than 5 years of industry experience. He specializes in technologies such as HTML5, CSS3, PHP, jQuery, Twitter Bootstrap, and SASS. He also has knowledge of CoffeeScript and AngularJS. In addition to web development, he has been involved in building training materials and writing tutorials for twenty19 (`http://www.twenty19.com/`) for the technologies mentioned previously.

Besides Packt Publishing, he has been associated with Apress and Manning Publications as a technical reviewer for several of their titles.

Taroon Tyagi is a dreamer, designer, and a solution architect for mobile platforms and the Web. He is a rationalistic optimist, with lust for food, technology, and knowledge. He has more than 5 years of professional and industrial experience in web, UX, UI design, and frontend development. He currently works as the Head of Design and Interaction at Fizzy Software Pvt. Ltd, based out of Gurgaon, India.

When online, he is constantly involved with web communities experimenting with new technologies and looking for inspiration. When offline, he enjoys music, books, wire-framing, and digging philosophy.

He worked as a technical reviewer for a few books published by Packt Publishing.

www.PacktPub.com

Support files, eBooks, discount offers, and more

For support files and downloads related to your book, please visit www.PacktPub.com.

Did you know that Packt offers eBook versions of every book published, with PDF and ePub files available? You can upgrade to the eBook version at www.PacktPub.com and as a print book customer, you are entitled to a discount on the eBook copy. Get in touch with us at service@packtpub.com for more details.

At www.PacktPub.com, you can also read a collection of free technical articles, sign up for a range of free newsletters and receive exclusive discounts and offers on Packt books and eBooks.

https://www2.packtpub.com/books/subscription/packtlib

Do you need instant solutions to your IT questions? PacktLib is Packt's online digital book library. Here, you can search, access, and read Packt's entire library of books.

Why subscribe?

- Fully searchable across every book published by Packt
- Copy and paste, print, and bookmark content
- On demand and accessible via a web browser

Free access for Packt account holders

If you have an account with Packt at www.PacktPub.com, you can use this to access PacktLib today and view 9 entirely free books. Simply use your login credentials for immediate access.

Table of Contents

Preface

Responsive web design has taken the web design industry by storm. It's not a trend but a norm; it is something that is now normally expected from a website. You might have read and come across many discussions about responsive web design on blogs, forums, Facebook, and Twitter. Likewise, you want your website to be responsive in order to make it presentable on any screen size. Hence, this is the book you are looking for.

This book teaches you how to build presentable, responsive websites through examples, tips, and best practices of code writing and project organization. Additionally, you will also learn how to use CSS preprocessors, LESS, and Sass, which allows you to compose leaner style rules.

What this book covers

Chapter 1, *Responsive Web Design*, looks at the basic principle behind responsive web design, explains the basic technicalities to build a responsive website and features a couple of responsive frameworks as well as the advantages of using one.

Chapter 2, *Web Development Tools*, helps you to prepare, install, and set up the software to run projects and build responsive websites.

Chapter 3, *Constructing a Simple Responsive Blog with Responsive.gs*, introduces the Responsive.gs framework and builds the HTML structure of a blog using several HTML5 elements and the Responsive.gs grid system.

Chapter 4, *Enhancing the Blog Appearance*, composes CSS style rules to enhance the blog's look and feel. You will also learn how to manage blog styles modularly with partial style sheets and to compile them together into a single style sheet with a compiler.

Chapter 5, *Developing a Portfolio Website with Bootstrap*, builds a portfolio website with the Bootstrap framework components, including the grid system, button, and form as the base. We also learn how to use Bower to manage project libraries.

Chapter 6, Polishing the Responsive Portfolio Website with LESS, explores and teaches us the use of several LESS features, such as nesting, variables, and mixins, to write leaner and reusable style rules and eventually to polish the responsive portfolio website.

Chapter 7, A Responsive Website for Business with Foundation, builds a responsive website for a startup business using the Foundation framework grid system and components.

Chapter 8, Extending Foundation, teaches how to use Sass and SCSS syntax, such as variables, mixins, and function, to write maintainable and reusable styles for the responsive startup website.

Appendix, Pop Quiz Answers, contains answers to the multiple choice pop quizzes you will find throughout the book.

What you need for this book

You need to have a basic understanding of HTML and CSS; at least, you should know what an HTML element is and how to style an HTML element with CSS in its fundamental form. Some degree of familiarity and experience with HTML5, CSS3, and command lines, though not essential, will be a great help to get the most out of this book. We will explain each step and all the techniques in full, along with some handy tips and references.

Furthermore, you will also need a computer running Windows, OS X, or Ubuntu; an Internet browser (preferably Google Chrome or Mozilla Firefox); and a code editor (in this book, we will use Sublime Text).

Who this book is for

Responsive Web Design by Example Beginner's Guide Second Edition teaches readers how to build presentable responsive websites through practical examples and guides readers through the process bit by bit with in-depth explanation. It is the perfect book for anyone who wants to learn and build responsive websites quickly up and running regardless of the reader's proficiency, that is, new or seasoned web designers.

Sections

In this book, you will find several headings that appear frequently (Time for action, What just happened?, Pop quiz, and Have a go hero).

To give clear instructions on how to complete a procedure or task, we use these sections as follows:

Time for action – heading

1. Action 1
2. Action 2
3. Action 3

Instructions often need some extra explanation to ensure they make sense, so they are followed with these sections:

What just happened?

This section explains the working of the tasks or instructions that you have just completed.

You will also find some other learning aids in the book, for example:

Pop quiz – heading

These are short multiple-choice questions intended to help you test your own understanding.

Have a go hero – heading

These are practical challenges that give you ideas to experiment with what you have learned.

Conventions

You will also find a number of text styles that distinguish between different kinds of information. Here are some examples of these styles and an explanation of their meaning.

Code words in text, database table names, folder names, filenames, file extensions, pathnames, dummy URLs, user input, and Twitter handles are shown as follows: "The `boxsizing.htc` file that comes with Responsive.gs will apply similar functionality as in the CSS3 `box-sizing` property."

A block of code is set as follows:

```
* {
  -webkit-box-sizing: border-box;
  -moz-box-sizing: border-box;
  box-sizing: border-box;
  *behavior: url(/scripts/boxsizing.htc);
}
```

When we wish to draw your attention to a particular part of a code block, the relevant lines or items are set in bold:

```
*  {
   -webkit-box-sizing: border-box;
   -moz-box-sizing: border-box;
   box-sizing: border-box;
   *behavior: url(/scripts/boxsizing.htc);
}
```

Any command-line input or output is written as follows:

```
cd \xampp\htdocs\portfolio
bower init
```

New terms and **important words** are shown in bold. Words that you see on the screen, in menus or dialog boxes for example, appear in the text like this: " Check the **Source Map** option for both style sheets to generate the source map files, which would help us when debugging."

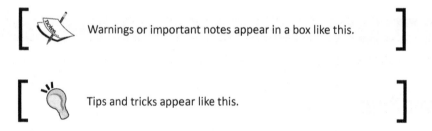

Warnings or important notes appear in a box like this.

Tips and tricks appear like this.

Reader feedback

Feedback from our readers is always welcome. Let us know what you think about this book—what you liked or disliked. Reader feedback is important for us as it helps us develop titles that you will really get the most out of.

To send us general feedback, simply e-mail feedback@packtpub.com, and mention the book's title in the subject of your message.

If there is a topic that you have expertise in and you are interested in either writing or contributing to a book, see our author guide at www.packtpub.com/authors.

Customer support

Now that you are the proud owner of a Packt book, we have a number of things to help you to get the most from your purchase.

Downloading the example code

You can download the example code files from your account at `http://www.packtpub.com` for all the Packt Publishing books you have purchased. If you purchased this book elsewhere, you can visit `http://www.packtpub.com/support` and register to have the files e-mailed directly to you.

Errata

Although we have taken every care to ensure the accuracy of our content, mistakes do happen. If you find a mistake in one of our books—maybe a mistake in the text or the code—we would be grateful if you could report this to us. By doing so, you can save other readers from frustration and help us improve subsequent versions of this book. If you find any errata, please report them by visiting `http://www.packtpub.com/submit-errata`, selecting your book, clicking on the **Errata Submission Form** link, and entering the details of your errata. Once your errata are verified, your submission will be accepted and the errata will be uploaded to our website or added to any list of existing errata under the Errata section of that title.

To view the previously submitted errata, go to `https://www.packtpub.com/books/content/support` and enter the name of the book in the search field. The required information will appear under the **Errata** section.

Piracy

Piracy of copyrighted material on the Internet is an ongoing problem across all media. At Packt, we take the protection of our copyright and licenses very seriously. If you come across any illegal copies of our works in any form on the Internet, please provide us with the location address or website name immediately so that we can pursue a remedy.

Please contact us at `copyright@packtpub.com` with a link to the suspected pirated material.

We appreciate your help in protecting our authors and our ability to bring you valuable content.

Questions

If you have a problem with any aspect of this book, you can contact us at `questions@packtpub.com`, and we will do our best to address the problem.

1
Responsive Web Design

I still remember, back when I was a kid, a mobile phone came with a mere tiny size monochromatic screen. All we could do at that time was make a phone call, text, and play a simple game. Today, mobile devices have drastically advanced in many ways.

New mobile devices are built with varying screen sizes; some even come with higher DPI or resolution. Most new mobile devices are now equipped with a touch-enabled screen, allowing us to interact with the device conveniently using a tap or a swipe of fingers. The screen orientation is switchable between portrait and landscape. The software is also more capable compared to older devices. The mobile browser, in particular, is now able to render and display web pages that are as good as a browser in a desktop computer.

In addition, the number of mobile users has exploded in the last couple of years. We can now see many people around spending countless hours facing their mobile devices, a phone, or a tablet, doing things such as running their businesses on the go or simple Internet browsing. The number of mobile users is likely to grow in the years to come and may even outnumber the total number of desktop users.

That is to say, mobiles have changed the Web and changed the way people use the Internet and enjoy websites. These advancements in mobile devices and the increasing mobile Internet usage prompts questions on a new paradigm to build websites that are accessible and function well in varying circumstances. This is where **Responsive Web Design** *comes in.*

In this chapter, we will cover the following topics:

◆ Glance at the basics of responsive web design, viewport meta tag, and CSS3 media queries

◆ Take a look at the responsive frameworks that we will use to build responsive websites in the following chapters

Responsive web design in a nutshell

Responsive web design is one of the most discussed topics in the web design and development community. So, I believe many of you have heard about it to a certain extent.

Ethan Marcotte was the one who coined the term "responsive web design". He suggests in his article *Responsive Web Design* (http://alistapart.com/article/responsive-web-design/), that the Web should seamlessly adjust and adapt to the environment where the users view the website rather than addressing it exclusively for a specific platform. In other words, the website should be responsive, it should be presentable on any screen size, regardless of the platform on which it is viewed.

Take the Time website (http://time.com/) as an example. The web page fits nicely on a desktop browser with a large screen size and also on a mobile browser with a limited viewable area. The layout shifts and adapts as the viewport size changes. As you can see in the following screenshot, on the mobile browser, the background color of the header is dark grey, the image is scaled down proportionally, and the Tap bar appears where Time hides the latest news, magazine, and videos sections:

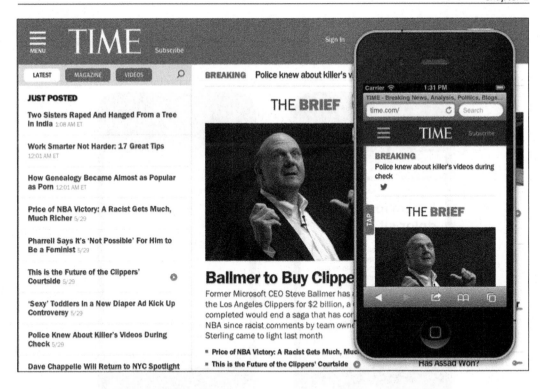

There are two components to build responsive websites, namely, **viewport meta tag** and **media queries**.

Viewport meta tag

Before smartphones, such as the iPhone, became mainstream, every website was built to be around 1000 px in width or 980 px wide and it was zoomed out to fit into the mobile phone screen, which eventually made the website unreadable. Hence, the <meta name="viewport"> was created.

In a nutshell, the viewport meta tag is used to define the web page scale and its visible area (viewport) in the browser. The following code is an example of a viewport meta tag in action:

```
<meta name="viewport" content="width=device-width, initial-scale=1">
```

The preceding viewport meta tag specification defines the web page viewport width to follow the device. It also defines the web page scale upon opening the web page for the first time at 1:1, in a way that the sizes and the dimensions of the web page content should be persistent; they should not be scaled up or scaled down.

In favor of comprehending how the viewport meta tag would affect a web page layout, I have created two web pages for comparison; one with the viewport meta tag added in and the other one without it. You can see the difference in the following screenshot:

The first website shown in the preceding image is issued with the viewport meta tag using the exact same specification as in our previous code example. As we have specified `width=device-width`, the browser acknowledges that the website viewport is at the same size as the device screen, so that it will not squish the web page to fit in the entire screen. The `initial-scale=1` will retain the title and the paragraph in their original size.

In the second website's example, as we did not add the viewport `meta` tag, the browser assumed that the web page should be displayed entirely. So, the browser forced the whole website down to fit within the whole screen area, making the title and the text totally unreadable.

A word on screen size and viewport

You may have found on many web design forums or blogs that viewport and screen size are mentioned interchangeably quite often. But, as a matter of fact, they are two different things.

Screen size refers to the device's actual screen size. A 13-inch laptop, for example, commonly has a screen size of 1280*800 pixels. The viewport, on the other hand, describes the viewable area in the browser where it displays websites. The following diagram illustrates this:

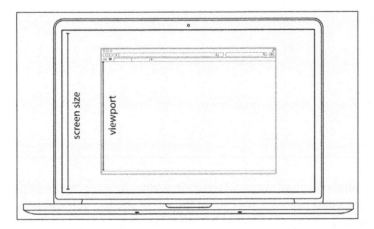

Media queries

The media types module in CSS enables us to target style rules to specific media. If you have created a print style sheet before, you certainly are familiar with the concept of media types. CSS3 introduced a new media type called media queries, which allow us to apply styles within the specified range of the viewport width, also known as breakpoints.

The following is one simple example; we decrease the p font size from 16px to 14px of the website when the website's viewport size is at 480px or lower.

```
p {
font-size: 16px;
}
@media screen and (max-width: 480px) {
p {
    font-size: 14px;
}
}
```

The following diagram illustrates the preceding code:

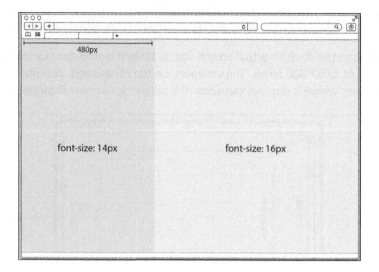

We can also combine multiple ranges of viewport widths by using the and operator. Following our preceding example, we can set the p font size to 14px when the viewport size is between 480px and 320px in the following manner:

```
@media screen and (min-width: 320px) and (max-width: 480px) {
p {
font-size: 11px;
  }
}
```

[**Viewport and media queries references**

We will be dealing with viewport meta tag and media queries while building responsive websites. Packt Publishing has published a dedicated book, *Responsive Web Design with HTML5 and CSS3, Ben Frein, Packt Publishing*, which covers these two in greater detail. I would like to suggest reading it as a companion and complement to this book.]

A look into responsive frameworks

Building a responsive website can be very tedious work. There are many measurements to be considered while building a responsive website, one of which would be creating the responsive grid.

The grid helps us build websites with proper alignment. If you have ever used 960. gs (`http://960.gs/`), which is one of the popular CSS frameworks, you would have experienced how easy it is to organize the web page layout by adding preset classes, such as `grid_1` or `push_1`, in the elements.

However, the 960.gs grid is set in a fixed unit, namely, pixel (`px`), which is not applicable when it comes to building a responsive website. We need a framework with the grid set in percentage (`%`) unit to build responsive websites; we need a responsive framework.

A responsive framework provides the building blocks to build responsive websites. Generally, it includes the classes to assemble a responsive grid, the basic styles for typography and form inputs, and a few styles to address various browser quirks. Some frameworks even go further with a series of styles to create common design patterns and web user interfaces such as buttons, navigation bars, and image slider. These predefined styles allow us to develop responsive websites faster with less hassle. The following are a few other reasons why using a responsive framework is a favorable option to build responsive websites:

- **Browser compatibility**: Assuring the consistency of a web page on different browsers is really painful and more distressing than developing the website itself. However, with a framework, we can minimize the work to address browser compatibility issues. The framework developers have most likely tested the framework on various desktop browsers and mobile browsers with the most constrained environment prior to releasing it publicly.

- **Documentation**: A framework, in general, also comes with comprehensive documentation that records the bits and pieces on using the framework. The documentation will be very helpful for entry users to begin studying the framework. It is also a great advantage when we are working with a team. We can refer to the documentation to get everyone on the same page and follow the standard code of writing conventions.

- **Community and extensions**: Some popular frameworks such as Bootstrap and Foundation have an active community that helps address the bugs in the framework and extends the functionality. The jQuery UI Bootstrap (`http://jquery-ui-bootstrap.github.io/jquery-ui-bootstrap/`) is perhaps a good example in this case. The jQuery UI Bootstrap is a collection styles for jQuery UI widgets to match the feel and look of Bootstrap's original theme. It's now common to find free WordPress and Joomla themes that are based on these frameworks.

Through the course of this book, we will be building three responsive websites by using three different responsive frameworks, namely Responsive.gs, Bootstrap, and Foundation.

The Responsive.gs framework

Responsive.gs (http://responsive.gs/) is a lightweight, responsive framework, which is merely 1 KB in size when compressed. Responsive.gs is based on a width of 940 px, and made in three variants of grids, that is, 12, 16, and 24 columns. What's more, Responsive.gs is shipped with box-sizing polyfill, which enables CSS3 box-sizing in Internet Explorer 6, 7, and 8, and makes it decently presentable in those browsers.

 Polyfill is a piece of code that enables certain web features and capabilities that are not built in the browser natively. Usually, it addresses the older versions of Internet Explorer. For example, you can use HTML5Shiv (https://github.com/aFarkas/html5shiv) so that new HTML5 elements, such as <header>, <footer>, and <nav>, are recognized in Internet Explorer 6, 7, and 8.

A word on CSS box model

HTML elements, which are categorized as block-level elements, are essentially boxes drawn with the content width, height, margin, padding, and border through CSS. Prior to CSS3, we were facing constraints when specifying a box. For instance, when we specify a <div> tag with a width and height of 100px, as follows:

```
div {
  width: 100px;
  height: 100px;
}
```

The browser will render div as a 100px square box, as shown in the next diagram:

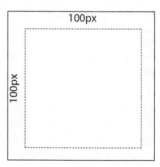

However, this will only be true if the padding and border have not been added in. As a box has four sides, a padding of 10px (padding: 10px;) will actually add 20px to the width and height—10px for each side, as shown in the following diagram:

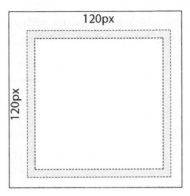

While it takes up space on the page, the element's margin space is reserved outside the element rather than as part of the element itself; thus, if we give an element a background color, the margin area will not take that color.

CSS3 box sizing

CSS3 introduced a new property called box-sizing, which lets us specify how the browser should calculate the CSS box model. There are a couple of values that we can apply within the box-sizing property.

Value	Description
content-box	This is the default value of the box model. This value specifies the padding and the border-box's thickness outside the specified width and height of the content, as we have demonstrated in the preceding section.
border-box	This value will do the opposite of what the content-box does; it includes the padding and the border box as the width and height of the box.
padding-box	At the time of writing this book, this value is experimental and has just been added recently. This value specifies the box dimensions.

In each of the projects in this book, we will be using the `border-box` value so that we can determine the box dimensions with ease for the websites. Let's take our preceding example to understand this, but this time we will set the `box-sizing` model to `border-box`. As mentioned in the preceding table, the `border-box` value will retain the box's width and the height as `100px`, regardless of the padding and border addition. The following illustration shows a comparison between the outputs of the two different values, `content-box` (the default value) and `border-box`:

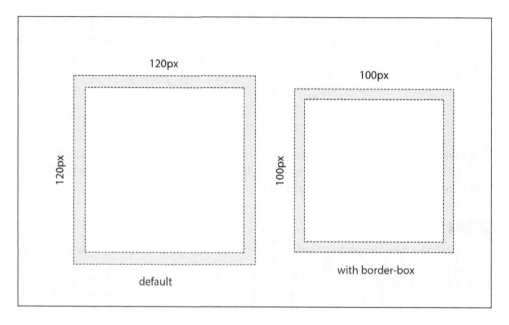

In this book, we will use Responsive.gs and explore more of it in the next two chapters to build a simple responsive blog.

The Bootstrap framework

Bootstrap (http://getbootstrap.com/) was originally built by Mark Otto (http://markdotto.com/) and initially intended only for internal use on Twitter. In short, Bootstrap was then launched for free for public consumption.

 Bootstrap has long been associated with Twitter, but since the author has departed from Twitter and Bootstrap itself has grown beyond his expectations, Bootstrap now stands on its own brand (http://blog.getbootstrap.com/2012/09/29/onward/).

If you refer to the initial development, the responsive feature was not yet added. It was then added in Version 2 due to the increasing demand for creating responsive websites.

Bootstrap also comes with many more added features as compared to Responsive.gs. It is packed with preset user interface styles, which comprise common user interfaces used on websites such as buttons, navigation bars, pagination, and forms, so you don't have to create them from scratch again when starting a new project. On top of that, Bootstrap is also powered with some custom jQuery plugins such as image slider, carousel, popover, and modal box.

You can use and customize Bootstrap in many ways. You can directly customize the Bootstrap theme and its components directly through the CSS style sheets, the Bootstrap customize and download page (http://getbootstrap.com/customize/), or the Bootstrap LESS variables and mixins, which are used to generate the style sheets.

In this book, we will go into Bootstrap in *Chapter 5*, *Developing a Portfolio Website with Bootstrap*, and *Chapter 6*, *Polishing the Responsive Portfolio Website with LESS*, to build a responsive portfolio website.

The Foundation framework

Foundation (http://foundation.zurb.com/) is a framework created by ZURB, a design agency based in California. Similar to Bootstrap, Foundation is not just a responsive CSS framework; it is shipped with a preset grid, components, and a number of jQuery plugins to present interactive features.

Some high-profile brands, such as McAfee (http://www.mcafee.com/common/privacy/english/slide.html), which is one of the most respectable brands for computer antivirus, have built their websites using Foundation.

The Foundation style sheet is powered by Sass, a Ruby-based CSS preprocessor. We will be discussing more about Sass, along with the Foundation features in the last two chapters of this book; therein, we will be developing a responsive website for a startup company.

There are many complaints that the code in responsive frameworks is excessive; as a framework such as Bootstrap is used widely, it has to cover every design scenario and thus, it comes with some extra styles that you might not need for your website. Fortunately, we can easily minimize this issue by using the right tools, such as CSS preprocessors, and following a proper workflow.

Frankly, there isn't a perfect solution; and using a framework certainly isn't for everyone. It all comes down to your needs, your website's needs, and in particular, your client's needs and budgets. In reality, you will have to weigh these factors to decide whether you will go with a responsive framework or not. Jem Kremer has an extensive discussion in this regard in her article *Responsive Design Frameworks: Just Because You Can, Should You?* (`http://www.smashingmagazine.com/2014/02/19/responsive-design-frameworks-just-because-you-can-should-you/`)

A brief introduction to CSS preprocessors

Both Bootstrap and Foundation use CSS preprocessors to generate their style sheets. Bootstrap uses LESS (`http://lesscss.org/`)—though the official support for Sass has just been released recently. Foundation, on the contrary, uses Sass as the only way to generate its style sheets (`http://sass-lang.com/`).

CSS preprocessor is not an entirely new language. If you have known CSS, you should be accustomed to the CSS preprocessor immediately. The CSS preprocessor simply extends CSS by allowing the use of programming features such as variables, functions, and operations.

The following is an example of how we write CSS with the LESS syntax:

```
@color: #f3f3f3;

body {
  background-color: @color;
}
p {
  color: darken(@color, 50%);
}
```

Downloading the example code

You can download the example code files from your account at `http://www.packtpub.com` for all the Packt Publishing books you have purchased. If you purchased this book elsewhere, you can visit `http://www.packtpub.com/support` and register to have the files e-mailed directly to you.

When the preceding code is compiled, it takes the `@color` variable that we have defined and places the value in the output, as follows:

```
body {
  background-color: #f3f3f3;
}
p {
  color: #737373;
}
```

The variable is reusable throughout the style sheet and this enables us to retain style consistency and make the style sheet more maintainable.

We are going to use and explore CSS preprocessors, LESS, and Sass further during the course of building responsive websites with Bootstrap (*Chapter 5, Developing a Portfolio Website with Bootstrap* and *Chapter 6, Polishing the Portfolio Website with LESS*) and Foundation (*Chapter 7, A Responsive Website for Business with Foundation*, and *Chapter 8, Extending Foundation*).

Have a Go Hero — delve into responsive web design

Our discussion on responsive web design here, though essential, is merely the tip of the iceberg. There is so much more about responsive web design than what we have recently covered in the preceding sections. I would suggest that you take your time to get yourself more insight and remove any apprehension on responsive web design, including the concept, the technicalities, and some constraints.

The following are some of the best recommendations for references:

♦ The *Responsive Web Design* article by Ethan Martcotte (`http://alistapart.com/article/responsive-web-design`), is where it all begins

♦ Also a good place to start is *Responsive Web Design* by Rachel Shillcock (`http://webdesign.tutsplus.com/articles/responsive-web-design--webdesign-15155`)

♦ *Don't Forget the Viewport Meta Tag* by Ian Yates (`http://webdesign.tutsplus.com/articles/quick-tip-dont-forget-the-viewport-meta-tag--webdesign-5972`)

♦ *How To Use CSS3 Media Queries To Create a Mobile Version of Your Website* by Rachel Andrew (`http://www.smashingmagazine.com/2010/07/19/how-to-use-css3-media-queries-to-create-a-mobile-version-of-your-website/`)

- Read about the future standards on responsive image using HTML5 Picture Element *Responsive Images Done Right: A Guide To <picture> And srcset* by Eric Portis (http://www.smashingmagazine.com/2014/05/14/responsive-images-done-right-guide-picture-srcset/)

- A roundup of methods to make data table responsive (http://css-tricks.com/responsive-data-table-roundup/)

Pop Quiz — responsive web design main components

Q1. In his article, which we have referred to about two times in this chapter, Ethan Marcotte mentioned the main technical ingredients that formulate a responsive website. What are those main components?

1. Viewport Meta Tag and CSS3 Media Queries.

2. Fluid grids, flexible images, and media queries.

3. Responsive images, breakpoints, and polyfills.

Q2. What is a viewport?

1. The screen size of the device.

2. The region where the web page is rendered.

3. The meta tag to set the web page's viewport size.

Q3. Which one of these is the correct way to declare CSS3 Media Queries?

1. `@media (max-width: 320px) { p{ font-size:11px; }}`

2. `@media screen and (max-device-ratio: 320px) { div{ color:white; }}`

3. `<link rel="stylesheet" media="(max-width: 320px)" href="core.css" />`

Responsive web design inspiration sources

Now, before we jump into the next chapters and start building responsive websites, it may be a good idea to spend some time looking for ideas and inspiration for responsive websites; to see how they are built and how the layout is organized on desktop browsers, as well as on mobile browsers.

It's a common thing for websites to be redesigned from time to time to stay fresh. So, instead of making a pile of website screenshots, which may no longer be relevant in the next several months because of the redesign, we're better going straight to the websites that curate websites, and the following are the places to go:

- MediaQueries (`http://mediaqueri.es/`)
- Awwwards (`http://www.awwwards.com/websites/responsive-design/`)
- CSS Awards (`http://www.cssawards.net/structure/responsive/`)
- WebDesignServed (`http://www.webdesignserved.com/`)
- Bootstrap Expo (`http://expo.getbootstrap.com/`)
- Zurb Responsive (`http://zurb.com/responsive`)

Summary

In this chapter, we glanced at the short story behind responsive web design, as well as the viewport meta tag and CSS3 media queries, which formulate responsive websites. This chapter also concluded that we are going to work on three projects by using the following frameworks: Responsive.gs, Bootstrap, and Foundation.

Using a framework is an easier and faster way to get responsive websites up and running, rather than building everything from scratch on our own. Alas, as mentioned, using a framework also has some negative aspects. If it is not done properly, the end result could all go wrong. The website could be stuffed and stuck with unnecessary styles and JavaScript, which at the end makes the website load slowly and hard to maintain.

We need to set up the right tools; not only will they facilitate the projects, but they will also help us in making the website more easy to maintain, and this is what we are going to do in the next chapter.

2
Web Development Tools

Every professional has a set of tools that facilitates their work and gets the job done. Likewise, we will also need our own tools to do our bit of building responsive websites. So, before we start working on the projects in this book, the following are the tools we have to prepare.

Tools that we will have to prepare include:

- A code editor for writing codes
- A compiler that will compile the CSS preprocessor syntax into plain CSS
- A local server to host the websites locally during the development stage
- A bower to manage the website libraries

Choosing a code editor

As soon as we start writing code for HTML, CSS, and JavaScript, we need a code editor. A code editor is an indispensible tool to develop websites. Technically, you will only need text editors such as TextEdit in OS X or Notepad in Windows to write and edit code. However, by using a code editor, your eyes will be less irritated.

Similar to Microsoft Word, which has been specially designed to make word and paragraph formatting more intuitive, a code editor is designed with a set of special features that improves code writing experiences such as syntax highlighting, auto-completion, code snippets, multiple line selection, and supporting a large number of languages. Syntax highlighting will display code in different colors, enhancing code readability and make it easy to find errors in the code.

My personal preference for a code editor, and the one that I will use in this book, is Sublime Text (`http://www.sublimetext.com/`). Sublime Text is a cross-platform code editor available for Windows, OS X, and Linux. It can be downloaded free for evaluation for an unlimited time.

 Keep in mind that while Sublime Text allows us to evaluate free of cost for an unlimited time, it may sometimes bug you to purchase the license. If you start feeling annoyed, please consider purchasing the license.

Sublime Text Package Control

One thing that I love most from Sublime Text is Package Control where we can search, install, list, and remove extensions from Sublime Text conveniently. However, Package Control does not come pre-installed with Sublime Text. So, assuming you have installed Sublime Text (which I think you should have), we will install Package Control in Sublime Text.

Time for action – installing Sublime Text Package Control

Perform the following steps to install Sublime Text Package Control; this will allow us to install Sublime Text extension easily:

1.   The easiest way to install Package Control in Sublime Text is through the Sublime Text console. Open the console by navigating to the **View | Console** menu in Sublime Text. You should now see a new input field show up at the bottom, as shown in the following screenshot:

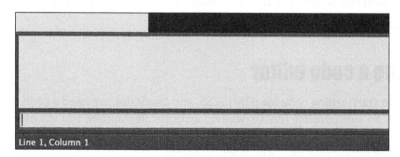

2.   Due to the overhaul made in Sublime Text 3 that changed almost the entire API, the Package Control is now separated in two versions, one for Sublime Text 2 and the other one for Sublime Text 3. Each version requires a different piece of code to install Package Control. If you are using Sublime Text 2, copy the code from `https://sublime.wbond.net/installation#st2`. If you are using Sublime Text 3, copy the code from `https://sublime.wbond.net/installation#st3` instead.

3. Paste the code that you have copied from step 2 into the console input field, as shown in the following screenshot:

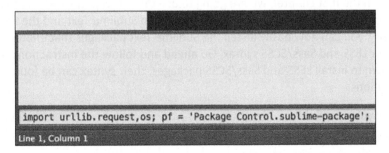

```
import urllib.request,os; pf = 'Package Control.sublime-package';
```
Line 1, Column 1

4. Press *Enter* to run the codes and eventually install Package Control. Keep in mind that the process may take a while depending on your Internet connection speed.

What just happened?

We just installed Package Control to search, install, list, and remove extensions in Sublime Text easily. You can access Package Control through **Command Palette...**, which can be accessed by navigating to the **Tools | Command Palette...** menu. Alternatively, you can press a key shortcut to access it faster. Windows and Linux users can press *Ctrl + Shift + P*, while OS X users can press *Command + Shift + P*. Then, search for **Command Palette...** to list all available commands for Package Control.

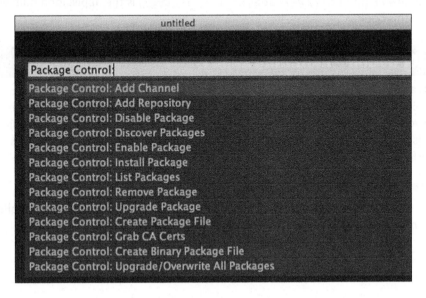

Have a go hero – install the LESS and Sass syntax-highlighting package

As mentioned in the first chapter, we are going to use these CSS preprocessors to compose styles in two of the projects in this book. Having installed Sublime Text and the Package Control already, you can now easily install the Sublime Text packages that enable color highlighting for LESS and Sass/SCSS syntax. Go ahead and follow the instructions that we have just shown to install LESS and Sass/SCSS packages, their syntax can be found at the following locations:

- LESS Syntax for Sublime Text (`https://github.com/danro/LESS-sublime`)
- Syntax Highlighting for Sass and SCSS (`https://github.com/P233/Syntax-highlighting-for-Sass`)

Setting up a local server

Having a local server set up and running on our computer is necessary while developing a website. When we use a local server to store our website, we will be able to access it through `http://localhost/` in the browsers, and we will also be able to access it on mobile phone browsers and tablets, which will not be possible when we run the website under `file:///` `protocol`. Besides, some scripts may only be functioning under the HTTP protocol (`http://`).

There are many applications that make setting up a local server a breeze with only a few clicks, and XAMPP (`https://www.apachefriends.org/`) is the application that we will be using in this book.

Time for action – installing XAMPP

XAMPP is available for Windows, OS X, and Linux. Download the installer from `https://www.apachefriends.org/download.html`; pick the installer in accordance with the platform you are using right now. Each platform will have a different installer with different extensions; Windows users will get `.exe`, OSX users will get `.dmg`, while Linux users will get `.run`. Perform the following steps to install XAMPP in Windows:

1. Launch the XAMPP `.exe` installer.
2. If the Windows User Account Control prompts **Do you want to allow the following program to make changes to this computer?** click on **Yes**.

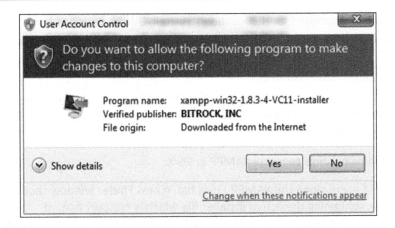

3. When the **XAMPP Setup Wizard** window appears, click on **Next** to start the setup.

4. XAMPP allows us to select which components to install. In this case, our web server requirement is the bare minimum. We will only need Apache to run the server, so we deselect the other options. (Note: the **PHP** option is grayed out; it cannot be unchecked):

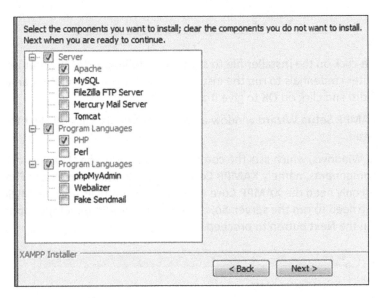

5. After confirming the components that will be installed, click on the **Next** button to proceed.

6. You will be prompted for the location to install XAMPP. Let's just leave it to the default location at `C:\xampp` and then click on **Next**.

7. Then, simply click on **Next** for the next two dialogs to start installing XAMPP. Wait until the process is complete.

8. When the process is complete, you should see the window stating **Setup has finished installing XAMPP**. Click on the **Finish** button to finalize the process and close the window.

Perform the following steps to install XAMPP in OS X:

1. For OS X users, open the XAMPP `.dmg` file. A new **Finder** window should appear, containing the actual installer file which is typically named `xampp-osx-*-installer` (the asterisk (*) represents the XAMPP version), as shown in the following screenshot:

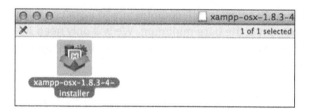

2. Double-click on the **installer** file to start the installation. XAMPP requires your computer credentials to run the installer. So, enter your computer name and password and click on **OK** to give it access.

3. The **XAMPP Setup Wizard** window appears afterwards; click on **Next** to start the setup.

4. Unlike Windows, which lists the components per item, the OS X version only shows two components, namely **XAMPP Core Files** and **XAMPP Developer Files**. Herein, we will only need the **XAMPP Core Files**, which comprises Apache, MySQL, and PHP that we need to run the server. So, deselect the **XAMPP Developer** option and then click on the **Next** button to proceed.

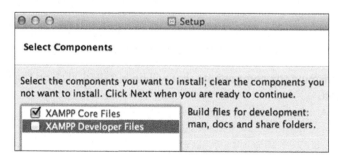

5. You will be prompted that XAMPP will be installed in the `Applications` folder. Unlike Windows, this directory can't be edited. So, click on **Next** to proceed.

6. Then, simply click on the **Next** button for the next two dialogs to start installing XAMPP. Wait until it is complete.

7. When the installation is complete, you will see **Setup has finished installing XAMPP** displayed in the window. Click on the **Finish** button to finalize the process and close the window.

Perform the following steps to install XAMPP in Ubuntu:

1. Download the XAMPP installer for Linux. The installer comes in the `.run` extension and is available for 32-bit and 64-bit systems.

2. Open the terminal and navigate to the folder where the installer is downloaded. Assuming it's in the `Downloads` folder, type:

   ```
   cd ~/Downloads
   ```

3. Make the `.run` installer file executable with `chmod u+x`, followed by the `.run` installer filename:

   ```
   chmod u+x xampp-linux-*-installer.run
   ```

4. Execute the file with the `sudo` command followed by the `.run` installer file location, as follows:

   ```
   sudo ./xampp-linux-x64-1.8.3-4-installer.run
   ```

5. The command from Step 4 will bring up the **XAMPP Setup Wizard** window. Click on **Next** to proceed, as shown in the following screenshot:

6. The installer lets you select which components to install on the computer. Similar to the OS X version, there are two components shown in the option: **XAMPP Core Files** (containing Apache, MySQL, PHP, and a bunch of other things to run the server) and **XAMPP Developer Files**. As we do not need **XAMPP Developer Files**, we can deselect it and then click on the **Next** button.

7. The installer will show you that it will install XAMPP in /opt/lampp. The folder location can't be customized. Just click on the **Next** button to proceed.

8. Click on the **Next** button for the next two dialog screens to install XAMPP.

What just happened?

We have just set up a local server in our computer with MAMP. You can now access the local server with the http://localhost/ address through the browsers. For OS X users, however, the address is your computer username followed by .local. Say that your username is john the local server is accessible through john.local. The local server directory path is different for each platform:

◆ In Windows: C:\xampp\htdocs
◆ In OSX: /Applications/XAMPP/htdocs

- In Ubuntu: `/opt/lampp/htdocs`

 Ubuntu users may want to change the permissions and create a `symlink` folder on the desktop to reach the `htdocs` folder conveniently. To do so, you can run the `sudo chown username:groupname /opt/lampp/htdocs` command through the terminal from the desktop location. Replace `username` and `groupname` to match your own.

The `ln -s /opt/lamp/htdocs` folder is where we will have to put our project folders and files. From now on, we will refer to this folder simply as `htdocs`. XAMPP is also equipped with a graphical application where you can turn the server on and off, as shown in the following screenshot:

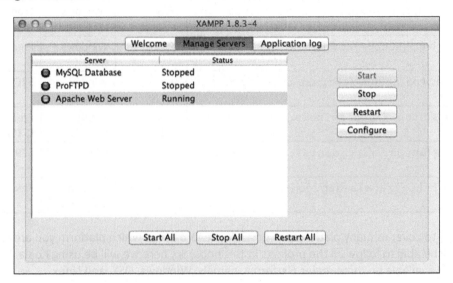

 Ubuntu users, you'll have to run `sudo /opt/lampp/manager-linux.run` or `manager-linux-x64.run`.

Choosing a CSS preprocessor compiler

As we will be using LESS and Sass to generate the style sheets of our responsive website, we will need a tool that will compile or change them into normal CSS format.

Back when CSS preprocessors were just gaining momentum, the only way to compile them was through command lines, which may have been the stumbling block for many people to even try CSS preprocessors at that time. Fortunately, we now have plenty of applications with a nice graphical interface to compile CSS preprocessors; the following is the list for your reference:

Tools	Language	Platform	Price
WinLESS (`http://winless.org/`)	LESS	Windows	Free
SimpLESS (`http://wearekiss.com/simpless`)	LESS	Windows, OSX	Free
ChrunchApp (`http://crunchapp.net`)	LESS	Windows, OSX	Free
CompassApp (`http://compass.handlino.com`)	Sass	Windows, OSX, Linux	$10
Prepros (`http://alphapixels.com/prepros/`)	LESS, Sass, and so on	Windows, OSX	Freemium ($24)
Codekit (`https://incident57.com/codekit/`)	LESS, Sass, and so on	OSX	$29
Koala (`http://koala-app.com/`)	LESS, Sass, and so on	Windows, OSX, Linux	Free

I will try to cover as many platforms as possible. Regardless of which platform you are using, you will be able to follow all the projects in this book. So, here we will be using Koala. It's free and available on three major platforms, namely, Windows, OSX, and Linux.

Installing Koala in each platform is pretty straightforward.

Browser for development

Ideally, we have to test our responsive websites in as many browsers as possible, including beta browsers such as Firefox Nightly (`http://nightly.mozilla.org/`) and Chrome Canary (`http://www.google.com/intl/en/chrome/browser/canary.html`). This is to ensure that our website is functioning well in different environments. However, during the development, we may pick one primary browser for development and as the point of reference of how the website should be put on display.

In this book, we will be using Chrome (`https://www.google.com/intl/en/chrome/browser/`). It is my humble opinion that Chrome, besides running fast, is also a very powerful web development tool. Chrome comes with a set of tools that are ahead of the other browsers. The following are two of my favorite tools in Chrome when it comes to developing responsive websites.

Source maps

One of the pitfalls of using CSS preprocessors is when debugging the style sheet. As the style sheet is generated and the browser refers to the CSS style sheet, we will find it hard to discover where exactly the code is declared within the CSS preprocessor's style sheet.

We may tell the compiler to generate comments containing the line numbers of where the code is actually written, but source maps solve this snag more elegantly. Rather than generating a bunch of comments that eventually pollute the style sheet, we can generate a `.map` file on compiling CSS preprocessors. Through this `.map` file, browsers such as Chrome, with source maps enabled, will be able to point directly to the source when we inspect an element, as shown in the following screenshot:

As you can see from the preceding screenshot, the Chrome DevTools shown on the left with source maps enabled refer directly to the `.less` files that allow us to debug the website with ease. Whereas, the source maps of the one shown on the right is disabled, so it refers to `.css`, and debugging the website would require a bit of struggle.

The source maps feature is, by default, enabled in the latest version of Chrome. So, make sure that your Chrome is up-to-date.

Mobile emulator

There isn't any substitution for testing a responsive website in a real device, a phone, or a tablet. Each device has its own merits; some factors, such as the screen dimension, the screen resolution, and the version of mobile browser, will affect your website displayed on the device. Yet, if that is not possible, we can use a mobile emulator as an alternative.

Chrome is also shipped with a mobile emulator that works out-of-the-box. This feature contains a number of presets for many mobile devices including iPhone, Nexus, and Blackberry. This feature not only emulates the device's user agent, it also turns on a number of device specifications, including the screen resolution, pixel ratio, viewport size, and touch screen. This feature can be extremely useful for debugging our responsive website early during development, without requiring an actual mobile device.

The mobile emulator is accessible through the **Emulation** tab of the Chrome DevTool **Console** drawer, as shown in the following screenshot:

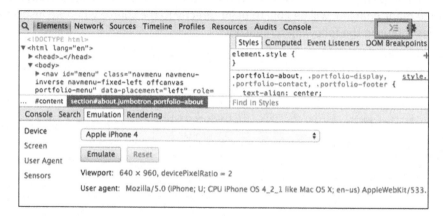

With the mobile emulator built into Chrome, we do not need to set up yet another emulator from a third-party application or Chrome extensions. Here, we will use it to test our responsive websites.

 Firefox has a similar feature to Chrome's mobile emulator, though it comparably only has very few features. You can enable this feature by navigating to the **Tools | Web Developer | Responsive Design View** menu.

Managing project dependency with Bower

We will need a number of libraries to manage a project dependency with Bower. In the web development context, we refer to a library as a collection of code, usually CSS and JavaScript, to add features on the website. Often, the website is dependent on a particular library for it to function its prime feature. As an example, if I built a website to convert currencies, the website will require Account.js (http://josscrowcroft.github.io/accounting.js/); it is a handy JavaScript library to convert regular numbers into currency format with the currency symbol.

It is common that we may add about five or more libraries on a single website, but maintaining all the libraries used in the website and making sure that they are all up-to-date could become cumbersome. This is where Bower is useful.

Bower (http://bower.io/) is a frontend package manager. It is a handy tool that streamlines the way we add, update, and remove libraries or dependencies (libraries that are required for the project) in our project. Bower is a Node.js module, so we first have to install Node.js (http://nodejs.org/) on our computer to be able to use Bower.

Time for action – installing Node.js

Perform the following steps to install Node.js in Windows, OS X, and Ubuntu (Linux). You may skip directly to the section of the platform you are using.

Perform the following steps to install Node.js in Windows:

1. Download the Node.js Windows installer from the Node.js download page (http://nodejs.org/download/). Choose your flavor for your Windows system, the 32-bit or 64-bit version, and the .msi or .exe installer.

32-bit or 64-bit

Follow this page to discover if your Windows computer is running on a 32-bit or a 64-bit system http://windows.microsoft.com/en-us/windows/32-bit-and-64-bit-windows.

2. Run the installer (.exe or .msi file).
3. Click on the **Next** button of the Node.js welcome message.
4. As usual, when you are installing a software or application, you will first be prompted by the application's license agreement. Once you have read the license, click on **I accept the terms in the License Agreement** and then click on the **Next** button to proceed.

5. Then, you will be prompted for the folder where Node.js should be installed. Leave it as the default folder, which is in `C:\Program Files\nodejs\`.

6. As you can see from the following screenshot, the installer then prompts to ask if you want to customize the item to be installed. Leave it as it is and click on the **Next** button to proceed, as shown in the following screenshot:

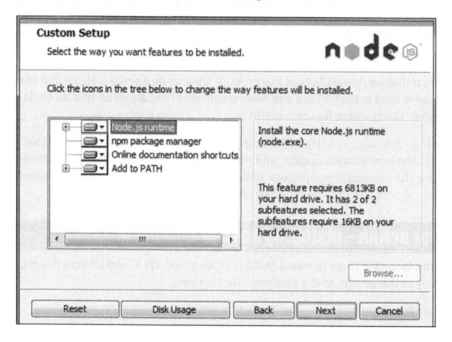

7. Afterwards, click on the **Install** button to start installing Node.js.

8. The installation process is quite fast; it takes only a few seconds. If you see the notification that says **Node.js has been successfully installed**, you may click on the **Finish** button to close the installation window.

Perform the following steps to install Node.js in OS X:

1. Download the Node.js installer for OS X, which comes in the `.pkg` extension.

2. The installer will show you a welcome message and show you the location where it will install Node.js (`/usr/local/bin`), as shown in the following screenshot:

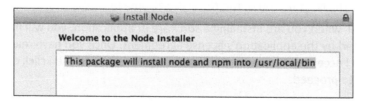

3. The installer then shows the user license agreement. If you read and agree to the license, click on the **Agree** button and then click on the **Next** button.

4. The Node.js installer for OS X allows you to select which Node.js feature to install prior to installing it into your computer. Here, we will install all the features; simply click on the **Install** button to start installing Node.js, as shown in the following screenshot:

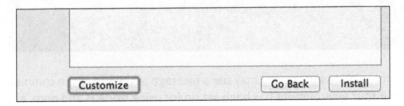

> If you want to customize your Node.js install, click on the **Customize** button at the bottom left, as shown in the previous screenshot.

Perform the following steps to install Node.js in Ubuntu:

Installing Node.js in Ubuntu is quite straightforward. Node.js can be installed through Ubuntu's **Advanced Packaging Tool** (**APT**) or `apt-get`. If you are using Ubuntu version 13.10 or the latest version, you can launch the terminal and run the following two commands consecutively:

```
sudo apt-get install nodejs
sudo apt-get install npm
```

If you are using Ubuntu version 13.04 or earlier, run the following command instead:

```
sudo apt-get install -y python-software-properties python g++ make
sudo add-apt-repository ppa:chris-lea/node.js
sudo apt-get update
sudo apt-get install nodejs
```

What just happened?

We have just installed Node.js and `npm` command, which enable us to use Bower later on through the **Node.js Package Manager** (**NPM**). The `npm` command line should now be accessible through the Windows command prompt or the OS X and Ubuntu terminals. Run the following command to test if the `npm` command works:

```
npm -v
```

This command returns the NPM version installed in the computer, as shown in the following screenshot:

Additionally, for Windows users, you may see a message at the top of the command prompt window saying **Your environment has been set up for using Node.js and npm**, as shown in the following screenshot:

This shows that you can perform the node and npm command within the command prompt. As we have set Node.js and npm is up and running, we are now going to install Bower.

Have a go hero – get yourself familiar with command lines

Throughout this book, we will be dealing with a number of command lines to install Bower, as well as Bower packages. Yet, if you are from a graphic design background like I was, where we mostly work on a graphical application, operating a command line for the first time could be really awkward and intimidating. Hence, I would suggest you take time and get yourself familiar with the basic command lines. The following are a few references worth checking out:

- *A Designer's Introduction to the Command Line* by Jonathan Cutrell (https://webdesign.tutsplus.com/articles/a-designers-introduction-to-the-command-line--webdesign-6358)

- *Navigating the Terminal: A Gentle Introduction* by Marius Masalar (https://computers.tutsplus.com/tutorials/navigating-the-terminal-a-gentle-introduction--mac-3855)

- *Introduction to the Windows Command Prompt* by Lawrence Abrams (`http://www.bleepingcomputer.com/tutorials/windows-command-prompt-introduction/`)

- *Introduction to Linux Command* by Paul Tero (`http://www.smashingmagazine.com/2012/01/23/introduction-to-linux-commands/`)

Time for action – installing Bower

Perform the following steps to install Bower:

1. If you are using Windows, open the command prompt. If you are using OS X or Ubuntu, open the terminal.

2. Run the following command:

   ```
   npm install -g bower
   ```

 If you are having trouble installing Bower in Ubuntu, run the command with `sudo`.

What just happened?

We have just installed Bower on the computer, which enables the `bower` command. The `-g` parameter that we included in the preceding command installs Bower globally, so that we are able to execute the `bower` command in any directory in the computer.

Bower commands

After installing Bower, we have access to a set of command lines to operate Bower functionalities. We will run these commands in the terminal, or in the command prompts if you are using Windows, just like we installed Bower with the `npm` command. All commands start with `bower` and are followed by the command keyword. The following is the list of commands that we may use frequently:

Command	Function
`bower install <library-name>`	Installs a library into the project. When we perform this function, Bower creates a new folder called `bower_components` to save all the library files.
`bower list`	Lists all installed package names in the project. This command also shows the new version if available.

Command	Function
`bower init`	Sets the project as the Bower project. This command also creates `bower.json`.
`bower uninstall <library-name>`	Removes the library name from the project.
`bower version <library-name>`	Retrieves the installed library version.

 You can run `bower --help` for the complete list of commands.

Pop quiz – web development tools and command lines

Q1. We have just installed Sublime Text along with Package Control. What is the Package Control used for?

1. To install and remove the Sublime Text package easily.

2. To install LESS and Sass/SCSS packages.

3. To manage packages in Sublime Text.

Q2. We have also installed XAMPP. Why did we need to install XAMPP?

1. To host the websites locally.

2. To develop websites locally.

3. To manage the project locally.

Summary

In this chapter, we have installed Sublime Text, XAMPP, Koala, and Bower. All these tools will facilitate us in building the websites. As we have got the tools prepared, we can now start working on the projects. So, let's move on to the next chapter and start the very first project.

3
Constructing a Simple Responsive Blog with Responsive.gs

In the previous chapter, we installed a number of software that will facilitate our projects. Here, we will start off our very first project. In this project, we are going to build a responsive blog.

Having a blog is essential for a company. Even several Fortune 500 companies such as FedEx (`http://outofoffice.van.fedex.com/`*), Microsoft (*`https://blogs.windows.com/`*) and General Motors (*`http://fastlane.gm.com/`*) have official corporate blogs. A blog is a great channel for the company to publish official news as well as to connect with their customers and the masses. Making the blog responsive is the way to go to make the blog more accessible to the readers who may access the site through a mobile device, such as a phone or tablet.*

As the blog that we are going to build in this first project will not be that complex, this chapter would be an ideal chapter for those who have just come across responsive web design.

So let's get started.

To sum up, in this chapter, we will cover the following topics:

- Dig into Responsive.gs components
- Examine the blog blueprint and design
- Organize the website files and folders
- Look into HTML5 elements for semantic markup
- Construct the blog markup

Responsive.gs components

As we mentioned in *Chapter 1*, *Responsive Web Design*, Responsive.gs is a lightweight CSS framework. It comes only with the bare minimum requirements for building responsive websites. In this section, we are going to see what is included in Responsive.gs.

The classes

Responsive.gs is shipped with a series of reusable classes to form the responsive grid that makes it easier and faster for web designers to build web page layout. These classes contain preset style rules that have been carefully calibrated and tested. So we can simply drop in these classes within the HTML element to construct the responsive grid. The following is a list of the classes in Responsive.gs:

Class name	Usage
container	We use this class to set the web page container and align it to the center of the browser window. This class, however, does not give the element width. Responsive.gs gives us the flexibility to set the width as per our requirement.
row, group	We use these two classes to wrap a group of columns. Both of these classes are set with so called self-clearing floats that fix some layout issues caused by the element with the CSS float property. Check the following references for further information about the CSS float property and the issue it may cause to a web page layout: ◆ *The Mystery Of The CSS Float Property* by Louis Lazaris (http://www.smashingmagazine.com/2009/10/19/the-mystery-of-css-float-property/) ◆ *All About Floats* by Chris Coyier (http://css-tricks.com/all-about-floats/)
col	We use this class to define the column of the web page. This class is set with the CSS float property. So any elements set with this class have to be contained within an element with the row or group class to avoid the issues caused by the CSS float property.
gutters	We use this class to add spaces between the columns set with the preceding col class.

Class name	Usage
span_{x}	This class defines the column width. So we use this class in tandem with the col class. Responsive.gs comes in three variants of grid, which gives us flexibility while organizing the web page layout. Responsive.gs is available in the 12-, 16-, and 24-columns format. These variants are set in three separate style sheets. If you download Responsive.gs package and then unpack it, you will find three style sheets named responsive.gs.12col.css, responsive.gs.16col.css, and responsive.gs.24col.css. The only difference between these style sheets is the number of span_ classes defined within it. It is apparent that the 24-column format style sheet has the most number of span_{x} classes; the class stretches from span_1 to span_24. If you need greater flexibility on dividing your page, then using the 24-column format of Responsive.gs is the way to go. Though each column may be too narrow.
clr	This class is provided to address the floating issue. We use this class in the occasion where using the row class would not be semantically appropriate.

Now, let's see how we apply them in an example to discover how they really work. Many times, you will see that a web page is divided into a multiple columns structure. Take that into account as our example here; we can do the following to construct a web page with two columns of content:

```
<div class="container">
<div class="row gutters">
  <div class="col span_6">
    <h3>Column 1</h3>
    <p>Lorem ipsum dolor sit amet, consectetur adipisicing
elit. Veniam, enim.</p>
  </div>
  <div class="col span_6">
    <h3>Column 2</h3>
    <p>Lorem ipsum dolor sit amet, consectetur adipisicing
elit. Reiciendis, optio.</p>
  </div>
</div>
</div>
```

As you can see from the preceding code snippet, we first added `container` that wraps all the contents. Then, it is followed by `div` with a `row` class to wrap the columns. At the same time, we also added the `gutters` class so that there will be blank space between the two columns. In this example, we used the 12-column format. Therefore, to split the page into two equal columns, we added the `span_6` class for each column. This is to say that the number of `span_{x}` classes should be equal to 12, 16, or 24 in accordance with the variant we are using in order for the columns to cover the entire container. So, if we used the 16-columns format, for example, we may add `span_8` instead.

In the browser, we will see the following output:

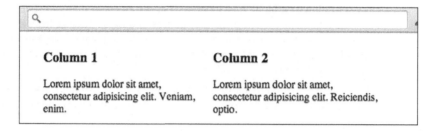

Using HTML5 elements for semantic markups

Paul Boag, in his article *Semantic code: What? Why? How?* (`http://boagworld.com/dev/semantic-code-what-why-how/`) wrote:

> *HTML was originally intended as a means of describing the content of a document, not as a means to make it appear visually pleasing.*

Unlike traditional content outlets such as newspapers or magazines, which are apparently intended for humans, the Web is read both by humans and machines such as search engines and screen readers that help visually impaired people navigate websites. So making our website structure semantic is really encouraged. Semantic markup allows these machines to understand the content better and also makes the content more accessible in different formats.

On that account, HTML5 introduces a bunch of new elements in its mission to make the web more semantic. The following is a list of elements that we are going to use for the blog:

Element	Description
`<header>`	The `<header>` element is used to specify the head of a section. While this element may be used commonly to specify the website header, it is also appropriate to use this element to specify, for example, the article header where we place the title and other supporting pieces of the article. We can use `<header>` multiple times in a single page where it is fitting.
`<nav>`	The `<nav>` element is used to represent a group of links that is intended as the primary navigation of the website or a section of a page.
`<article>`	The `<article>` element is quite self-explanatory. This element specifies the article of a website, such as the blog entry or the main page content.
`<main>`	The `<main>` element defines the main portion of a section. This element can be used to do things such as wrapping the article content.
`<figure>`	The `<figure>` element is used to specify document figures such as diagrams, illustrations, and images. The `<figure>` element can be used along with `<figcaption>` to add the figure's caption, if needed.
`<figcaption>`	As mentioned, `<figcaption>` represents the caption of the document's figure. Thus, it must be used in tandem with the `<figure>` element.
`<footer>`	Similar to the `<header>` element, the `<footer>` element is commonly used to specify the website footer. But it can also be used to represent the end or the lowest part of a section.

 Refer to the cheat sheet `http://websitesetup.org/html5-cheat-sheet/`, to find more new HTML elements in HTML5.

HTML5 search input types

Besides the new elements, we will also add one particular new type of input on the blog, search. As the name implies, the search input type is used to specify a search input. In the desktop browsers, you may not see a significant difference. You may also not immediately see how the search input type give advantages to the website and the users.

The search input type will boost the experience of mobile users. Mobile platforms such as iOS, Android, and the Windows Phone have been equipped with contextual screen keyboards. The keyboard will change according to the input type. You can see in the following screenshot that the keyboard displays the **Search** button, which allows users to perform a search more conveniently:

HTML5 placeholder attribute

HTML5 introduced a new attribute named `placeholder`. The specs described this attribute as a short hint (a word or short phrase) intended to aid the user with data entry when the control has no value, as shown in the following example:

```
<input type="search" name="search_form " placeholder="Search here…">
```

You will see that **Search here...** in the `placeholder` attribute is shown in the input field, as shown in the following screenshot:

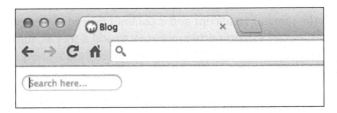

In the past, we relied on JavaScript to achieve a similar effect. Today, with the `placeholder` attribute, the application gets much simpler.

HTML5 in Internet Explorer

These new HTML elements make our document markup more descriptive and meaningful. Unfortunately, Internet Explorer 6, 7, and 8 will not recognize them. Thus, the selectors and style rules that address these elements are inapplicable; it is as if these new elements are not included in the Internet Explorer dictionary.

This is where a polyfill named HTML5Shiv comes into play. We will include HTML5Shiv (`https://github.com/aFarkas/html5shiv`) to make Internet Explorer 8 and its lower versions acknowledge these new elements. Read the following post (`http://paulirish.com/2011/the-history-of-the-html5-shiv/`) by Paul Irish for the history behind HTML5Shiv; how it was invented and developed.

Furthermore, older Internet Explorer versions won't be able to render the content in the HTML5 `placeholder` attribute. Fortunately, we can patch mimic the `placeholder` attribute functionality in the old Internet Explorer with a polyfill (`https://github.com/UmbraEngineering/Placeholder`). We will use it later on the blog as well.

A look into polyfills in the Responsive.gs package

Responsive.gs is also shipped with two polyfills to enable certain features that are not supported in Internet Explorer 6, 7, and 8. From now on, let's refer to these browser versions as "old Internet Explorer", shall we?

Box sizing polyfills

The first polyfill is available through an **HTML Component (HTC)** file named `boxsizing.htc`.

An HTC file is much the same as JavaScript and is commonly used in tandem with the Internet Explorer proprietary CSS property `behavior` to add a specific functionality to Internet Explorer. The `boxsizing.htc` file that comes with Responsive.gs will apply a similar functionality as in the CSS3 `box-sizing` property.

Responsive.gs includes the `boxsizing.htc` file within the style sheets as follows:

```
* {
  -webkit-box-sizing: border-box;
  -moz-box-sizing: border-box;
  box-sizing: border-box;
  *behavior: url(/scripts/boxsizing.htc);
}
```

As shown in the preceding code snippet, Responsive.gs applies the `box-sizing` property and includes the `boxsizing.htc` file with the asterisk selector. This asterisk selector is also known as wildcard selector; it selects all the elements within the document, and that being said, `box-sizing`, in this case, will affect all elements within the document.

> The `boxsizing.htc` file path must be an absolute path or relative to the HTML document in order for polyfill to work. This is a hack. It is something we forcibly use to make old Internet Explorer behave like a modern browser. Using an HTC file such as the preceding one is not considered valid as per the W3C standards.
>
> Please refer to this page by Microsoft regarding HTC files (`http://msdn.microsoft.com/en-us/library/ms531018(v=vs.85).aspx`).

CSS3 media queries polyfill

The second polyfill script that comes along with Responsive.gs is `respond.js` (`https://github.com/scottjehl/Respond`), which will "magically enable" CSS3 `respond.js` to work out of the box. There is no need for configuration; we can simply link the script within the `head` tag as follows:

```
<!--[if lt IE 9]>
<script src="respond.js"></script>
<![endif]-->
```

In the preceding code, we encapsulated the script inside `<!--[if lt IE 9]>` to make the script load only within the old Internet Explorer.

Examining the blog's wireframe

Building a website is much the same as building a house; we need to examine the specification of every corner before we stack up all the bricks. So, before we jump in to building the blog, we will examine the blog's wireframe to see how the blog is laid out and also see the things that will be displayed on the blog.

Let's take a look at the following wireframe. This wireframe shows the blog layout when it is viewed on the desktop screen:

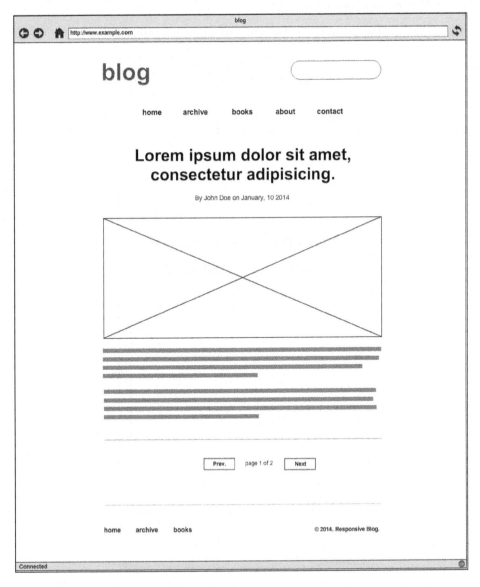

As you can see in the preceding screenshot, the blog will be plain and simple. In the header, the blog will have a logo and a search form. Down below the header, consecutively, we will place the menu navigation, the blog post, the pagination for navigating to the next or previous list of posts, and the footer.

The blog post, as in general, will comprise the title, the publishing date, the post's featured image, and the post excerpt. This wireframe is an abstraction of the blog's layout. We use it as our visual reference of how the blog layout will be arranged. So, in spite of the fact that we have shown only one post within the preceding wireframe, we will actually add a few more post items on the actual blog later on.

The following is the blog layout when the viewport width is squeezed:

When the viewport width gets narrow, the blog layout adapts. It is worth noticing that when we shift the layout, we should not alter the content flow as well as the UI hierarchy. Assuring the layout consistency between the desktop and the mobile version will help the users get familiar with a website quickly, regardless of where they are viewing the website. As shown in the preceding wireframe, we still have the UI set in the same order, albeit, they are now stacked vertically in order to fit in the limited area.

One thing that is worth mentioning from this wireframe is that the navigation turns into an HTML dropdown selection. We will discuss how to do so during the course of building the blog.

Now, as we have prepared the tools and checked out the blog layout, we are ready to start off the project. We will start off by creating and organizing the project directories and assets.

Organizing project directories and files

Often, we will have to link to certain files, such as style sheets and images. Unfortunately, websites are not a clever thing; they cannot find these files on their own. So, we must set the filepath correctly to avoid broken link errors.

This is why having organized directories and files is essential when it comes to building websites. It will be exceptionally important when we are working on a very large project with a team of people and with dozens to hundreds of files to handle. Poorly managed directories could drive anyone in the team insane.

Having well-organized directories will help us minimize potential errors of broken links. It will also make the project more maintainable and easily scalable in the future.

Time for action – creating and organizing project directories and assets

Perform the following steps to set up the project's working directory:

1. Go to the `htdocs` folder. As a reminder, this folder is the folder in the local server located at:

   - `C:\xampp\htdocs` in Windows
   - `/Applications/XAMPP/htdocs` in OSX
   - `/opt/lampp/htdocs` in Ubuntu

2. Create a new folder named `blog`. From now on, we will refer to this folder as the project directory.

3. Create a new folder named `css` to store style sheets.

4. Create a new folder named `image` to store images.

5. Create a new folder named `scripts` to store JavaScript files.

6. Create a new file named `index.html`; this HTML file will be the main page of the blog. Download the Responsive.gs package from `http://responsive.gs/`. The package comes in the `.zip` format. Extract the package to unleash the files within the package. There, you will find a number of files, including style sheets and JavaScript files, as you can see from the following screenshot:

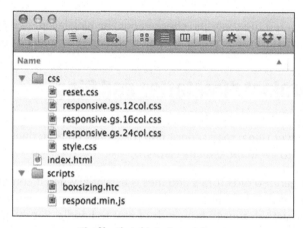

The files that ship in Responsive.gs

7. Move `responsive.gs.12col.css` to the `css` folder of the project directory; it is the only style sheet of Responsive.gs that we need.

8. Move `boxsizing.htc` to the `scripts` folder of the project directory.

9. The `respond.js` file that ships in the Responsive.gs package is out-of-date. Let's download the latest version of Respond.js from the GitHub repository (`https://github.com/scottjehl/Respond/blob/master/src/respond.js`) instead, and put it in the `scripts` folder of the project directory.

10. Download HTML5Shiv from `https://github.com/aFarkas/html5shiv`. Put the JavaScript file `html5shiv.js` within the `scripts` folder.

11. We will also use the placeholder polyfill that is developed by James Brumond (`https://github.com/UmbraEngineering/Placeholder`). James Brumond developed four different JavaScript files for cater to different scenarios.

12. The script that we are going to use here is `ie-behavior.js`, because this script specifically addresses Internet Explorer. Download the script (`https://raw.githubusercontent.com/UmbraEngineering/Placeholder/master/src/ie-behavior.js`) and rename it as `placeholder.js` to make it more apparent that this script is a placeholder polyfill. Put it in the `scripts` folder of the project directory.

13. The blog will need a few images to use as the post's featured image. In this book, we will use the images shown in the following screenshot, consecutively taken by Levecque Charles (`https://twitter.com/Charleslevecque`) and Jennifer Langley (`https://jennifer-langley.squarespace.com/photography/`):

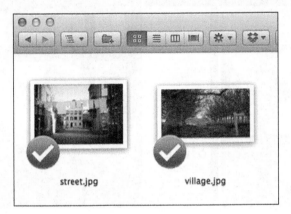

 Find more free high-definition images at Unsplash (`http://unsplash.com/`).

14. We will add a favicon to the blog. A favicon is a tiny icon that appears on the browser tab beside the title, which will be helpful for readers to quickly identify the blog. The following is a screenshot that shows a number of pinned tabs in Chrome. I bet that you are still able to recognize the websites within these tabs just by seeing the favicon:

Google Chrome pinned tabs

15. Further, we will also add the iOS icon. In Apple devices such as iPhone and iPad, we can pin websites on the home screen to make it quick to access the website. This is where the Apple icon turns out to be useful. iOS (the iPhone/iPad operating system) will show the icon we provide, as shown in the following screenshot, as if it was a native application:

Website added to the iOS home screen

16. These icons are provided in the source files that come along with this book. Copy these icons and paste them in the image folder that we have just created in step 5, as shown in the following screenshot:

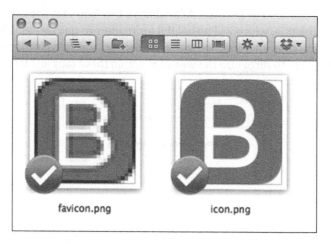

Create favicons and iOS icons quickly and easily with AppIconTemplate. AppIconTemplate (`http://appicontemplate.com/`) is a Photoshop template that makes it easy for us to design the icon. The template is also shipped with Photoshop Actions to generate the icons with a few clicks.

What just happened?

We have just created a directory for this project and put a couple of files in the directory. These files include the Responsive.gs style sheets and JavaScript files, images and icons, and a number of polyfills. We have also created an `index.html` file that will be the home page for the blog. At this point, the project directory should contain files as shown in the following screenshot:

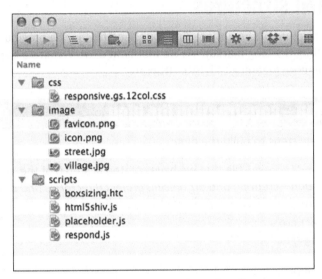

The current files and folders in the working directory

Have a go hero – making the directory structure more organized

Many people have their own preferences for how to organize their project's directory structure. The one shown in the previous section was just an example, of how I personally manage the directory for this project.

Try going further to make the directory more organized and meet your own preference for organization. A few common ideas are as follows:

* Make the folder name shorter, that is, `js` and `img`, instead of JavaScript and Image
* Group the folders `js`, `img`, and `css` all together in a new folder named `assets`

Pop quiz – using polyfill

Earlier in this book, we discussed polyfill and also mentioned a few polyfill scripts that we are going to implement in the blog.

Q1. When do you think would be an appropriate time to use the polyfill?

1. When the blog is viewed in Internet Explorer 6.
2. When the feature is not supported in the browser.
3. When we need to add new feature on the website.
4. We can use it at anytime.

The blog HTML structures

We have laid the structure of the project directories and files in the previous section. Let's now start constructing the blog markup. As we mentioned, we will use a number of HTML5 elements to form a more meaningful HTML structure.

Time for action – constructing the blog

Perform the following steps to build the blog:

1. Open the `index.html` file that we have created in step 6 of the previous section *Time for action – creating and organizing project directories and assets*. Let's start by adding the most basic HTML5 structure as follows:

```html
<!DOCTYPE html>
<html lang="en">
<head>
  <meta charset="UTF-8">
  <title>Blog</title>
</head>
<body>

</body>
</html>
```

Here, set DOCTYPE, which has been brought to the bare minimum form. The DOCTYPE format in HTML5 is now shorter and cleaner than the DOCTYPE format of its HTML4 counterpart. Then, we set the language of our page, which in this case is set to en (English). You may change it to your local language; find the code for your local language at http://en.wikipedia.org/wiki/List_of_ISO_639-1_codes.

We have also set the character encoding to `UTF-8` to enable the browser to render the Unicode characters, such as `U+20AC`, to the readable format €.

2. Below the `charset` meta tag in the `head` tag, add the following meta:

```
<meta http-equiv="X-UA-Compatible" content="IE=edge">
```

Internet Explorer can sometimes behave oddly, where it suddenly switches to compatibility mode and renders the page as viewed in Internet Explorer 8 and 7. This meta tag addition will prevent that from happening. It will force Internet Explorer to render the page with the highest support of the latest standards available in Internet Explorer.

3. Below the `http-equiv` meta tag, add the following meta viewport tag:

```
<meta name="viewport" content="width=device-width, initial-scale=1">
```

As we mentioned in *Chapter 1, Responsive Web Design*, the preceding viewport meta tag specification defines the web page viewport width to follow the device viewport size. It also defines the web page scale at 1:1 upon opening the web page the first time.

4. Link the Apple icon with the `link` tag, as follows:

```
<link rel="apple-touch-icon" href="image/icon.png">
```

As per Apple's official instructions, you would normally need to include multiple sources of icons to cater to iPhone, iPad, and the devices with a Retina screen. That isn't actually necessary for our blog. The trick is that we deliver the largest size required, which is 512 px square, through a single source, as shown in the previous screenshot.

Head over to the Apple documentation, specifying a web page icon for Web Clip (`https://developer.apple.com/library/ios/documentation/AppleApplications/Reference/SafariWebContent/ConfiguringWebApplications/ConfiguringWebApplications.html`), for further reference.

5. Add a description meta tag below the title, as follows:

```
<meta name="description" content="A simple blog built using Responsive.gs">
```

6. This description of the blog will show up in **Search Engine Result Page (SERP)**. In this step, we will construct the blog header. First, let's add the HTML5 `<header>` element along with the classes for styling, to wrap the header content. Add the following within the `body` tag:

```
<header class="blog-header row">

</header>
```

7. Within the `<header>` element that we added in step 9, add a new `<div>` element with the `container` and `gutters` class, as follows:

```
<header class="blog-header row">
<div class="container gutters">

</div>
</header>
```

Referring to the table shown earlier in the chapter, the `container` class will align the blog header content to the center of the browser window, while the `gutters` class will add spaces between the columns, which we will add in the next steps.

8. Create a new column to contain the blog logo/name with a `<div>` element along with the Responsive.gs `col` and `span_9` class to set the `<div>` element as column and specify the width. Don't forget to add the class to add custom styles:

```
<header class="blog-header row">
<div class="container gutters">
        <div class="blog-name col span_9">
<a href="/">Blog</a>
</div>
</div>
</header>
```

9. Referring to the blog wireframe, we will have a search form next to the blog logo/ name. On that account, create another new column with a `<div>` element together with the `col` and `span_3` class of Responsive.gs, and the input search type. Add the `<div>` element below the logo markup as follows:

```
<header class="blog-header row">
<div class="container gutters">
        <div class="blog-name col span_9">
    <a href="/">Blog</a>
</div>
<div class="blog-search col span_3">
        <div class="search-form">
            <form action="">
  <input class="input_full" type="search"      placeholder="Search
here...">
```

```
        </form>
                    </div>
        </div>
    </div>
    </header>
```

As we mentioned earlier in this chapter, we used an input search type to serve a better user experience. This input will show the mobile screen keyboard with a special key that allows users to hit the **Search** button and immediately run the search. We also added placeholder text with the HTML5 `placeholder` attribute to show the users that they can perform a search in the blog through the input field.

10. After constructing the header blog, we will construct the blog navigation. Here we will use the HTML5 `nav` element to define a new section as navigation. Create a `nav` element along with the supporting classes to style. Add the `nav` element below the header construction as follows:

```
...
</div>
</header>
<nav class="blog-menu row">

</nav>
```

11. Inside the `nav` element, create a `div` element with the `container` class to align the navigation content to the center of the browser window:

```
<nav class="blog-menu">
<div class="container">
</div>
</nav>
```

12. In accordance to the wireframe, the blog will have five items on the link menu. We will lay out this link with the `ul` element. Add the links within the container, as shown in the following code snippet:

```
<nav class="blog-menu row">
   <div class="container">
        <ul class="link-menu">
          <li><a href="/">Home</a></li>
          <li><a href="#">Archive</a></li>
          <li><a href="#">Books</a></li>
          <li><a href="#">About</a></li>
          <li><a href="#">Contact</a></li>
      </ul>
</div>
</nav>
```

13. Having done with constructing the navigation, we will construct the content section of the blog. Following the wireframe, the content will consist a list of posts. First, let's add the HTML5 `<main>` element to wrap the content below the navigation as follows:

```
...
</ul>
</nav>
<main class="blog-content row">

</main>
```

We use the `<main>` element as we consider the posts as the prime section of our blog.

14. Similar to the other blog sections¾the header and the navigation¾we add a container `<div>` to align the blog posts to the center. Add this `<div>` element within the `<main>` element:

```
<main class="blog-content row">
   <div class="container">

</div>
</main>
```

15. We will now create the blog post markup. Think of the blog post as an article. Thus, here we will use the `<article>` element. Add the `<article>` element within the container `<div>` that we will add in step 17 as follows:

```
<main class="blog-content row">
<div class="container">
   <article class="post row">

   </article>
</div>
</main>
```

16. As mentioned, the `<header>` element is not limited to define a header. The blog can be used to define the head of a section. In this case, apart from the blog header, we will use the `<header>` element to define the articles head section that contains the article title and publishing date.

17. Add the `<header>` element within the article element:

```
<article class="post row">
<header class="post-header">
<h1 class="post-title">
<a href="#">Useful Talks &amp; Videos for Mastering CSS</a>
   </h1>
        <div class="post-meta">
```

```
     <ul>
        <li class="post-author">By John Doe</li>
        <li class="post-date">on January, 10 2014</li>
     </ul>
     </div>
  </header>
  </article>
```

18. A picture is worth a thousand words. So, it's the norm to use an image to support the post. Here, we will display the image below the post header. We will group the featured image together with the post excerpt as the post summary, as shown in the following code:

```
...
 </header>
 <div class="post-summary">
 <figure class="post-thumbnail">
 <img src="image/village.jpg" height="1508" width="2800" alt="">
 </figure>
 <p class="post-excerpt">Lorem ipsum dolor sit amet,   consectetur
 adipisicing elit. Aspernatur, sequi, voluptatibus, consequuntur
 vero iste autem aliquid qui et rerum vel ducimus ex enim
 quas!...<a href="#">Read More...</a></p>
    </div>
 </article>
```

Add a few more posts subsequently. Optionally, you may exclude the post featured image in the other posts.

19. After adding a pile of posts, we will now add the post pagination. The pagination is a form of common page navigation that allows us to jump to the next or previous list of posts. Normally, the pagination is located at the bottom of the page after the last post item.

The pagination of a blog consists of two links to navigate to the next and previous page, and a small section to place the page numbers to show what page the user is currently in.

20. So, add the following code after the last post:

```
...
</article>
<div class="blog-pagination">
<ul>
   <li class="prev"><a href="#">Prev. Posts</a></li>
   <li class="pageof">Page 2 of 5</li>
   <li class="next"><a href="#">Next Posts</a></li>
</ul>
</div>
```

21. Finally, we will construct the blog footer. We can define the blog footer using the HTML5 `<footer>` element. The footer structure is identical to the one for the header. The footer will have two columns; each respectively contains the blog footer links (or, as we call it, secondary navigation) and copyright statement. These columns are wrapped with a `<div>` container. Add the following footer in the main section, as follows:

```
    ...
</main>
<footer class="blog-footer row">
   <div class="container gutters">
      <div class="col span_6">
<nav id="secondary-navigation"  class="social-   media">
         <ul>
            <li class="facebook">
<a href="#">Facebook</a>
  </li>
            <li class="twitter">
<a href="#">Twitter</a></li>
            <li class="google">
<a href="#">Google+</a>
   </li>
         </ul>
       </nav>
     </div>
   <div class="col span_6">
<p class="copyright">&copy; 2014. Responsive  Blog.</p>
   </div>
   </div>
</footer>
```

What just happened?

We have just finished constructing the blog's HTML structure¾the header, the navigation, the content, and the footer. Assuming that you have been following our instructions closely, you can access the blog at `http://localhost/blog/` or `http://{coputer-username}.local/blog/` in OS X.

However, as we haven't applied any styles, you will find that the blog is looking plain and the layout is yet to be organized:

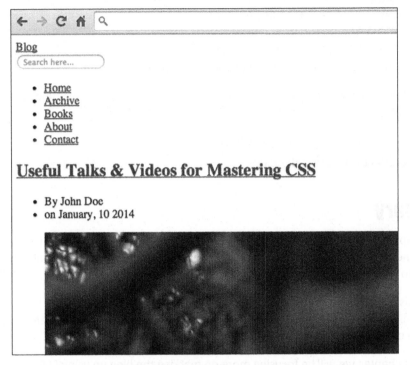

The blog appearance at the current stage

We will style the blog in the next chapter.

Have a go hero – creating more blog pages

In this book, we only build the blog's home page. However, you are free to extend the blog by creating more pages, such as adding an about page, a single post content page, and a page with a contact form. You may reuse the HTML structure that we have built in this chapter. Remove anything within the `<main>` element and replace it with content as per your requirement.

Pop quiz – HTML5 elements

Let's end this chapter with simple questions regarding HTML5:

Q1. What is the `<header>` element used for?

1. It is used to represent the website header.
2. It is used to represent a group of introductory and navigational aids.

Q2. What is the `<footer>` element used for?

1. It is used to represent the website footer.

2. It is used to represent the end or the lowest part of a section.

Q3. Is it allowed to use the `<header>` and `<footer>` elements multiple times within a single page?

1. Yes, as long as it's semantically logical.

2. No, it's considered redundant.

Summary

In this chapter, we started our first project. Earlier in the chapter, we explored the Responsive. gs components, looked into how Responsive.gs constructs a responsive grid, and what classes are used to shape the grid.

We also discussed HTML5, including the new elements, namely, the polyfills to mimic HTML5 features in the browsers that do not support particular features natively. Then, we used HTML5 to construct the blog markup.

In the next chapter, we will be focusing more on marking the blog up using CSS3 and adding some JavaScript. We will also be debugging the blog for errors that turn up in old Internet Explorer.

4
Enhancing the Blog Appearance

In the previous chapter, we constructed the blog markup from the header section to the footer section using HTML5 elements. The blog, however, is currently faceless. If you opened the blog in a browser, you will just see it bare; we have not yet written the styles that add up to its appearance.

Throughout the course of this chapter, we will focus on decorating the blog with CSS and JavaScript. We will be using CSS3 to add the blog styles. CSS3 brings a number of new CSS properties, such as `border-radius`, `box-shadow`, *and* `box-sizing`, *that allow us to decorate websites without the need to add images and extra markup.*

However, the CSS properties, as mentioned previously, are applicable only within the latest browser versions. Internet Explorer 6 to 8 are not able to recognize those CSS properties, and won't be able to output the result in the browsers. So, as an addition, we will also utilize a number of polyfills to make our blog presentable in the old Internet Explorer.

It's going to be an adventurous chapter. Let's go.

In this chapter, we shall cover the following topics:

- Looking into CSS3 properties and CSS libraries, which we are going to use in the blog
- Compile and minify style sheets and JavaScripts with Koala
- Compose the blog style rules with the mobile-first approach
- Optimize the blog for desktop
- Patch the blog in Internet Explorer with polyfills

Using CSS3

CSS3 ships with long-awaited properties, `border-radius` and `box-shadow`, that simplify old and tedious methods that were used to present rounded corner and drop shadow in HTML. On top of that, it also brings a new type of pseudo-element that enables us to style the placeholder text shown in input fields through the HTML5 `placeholder` attribute.

Let's take a look at how they work.

Creating rounded corners with CSS3

Back in the 90s, creating a rounded corner was complicated. Adding a pile of HTML markup, slicing out images, and formulating multiple line style of rules is inevitable, as presented in the post by Ben Ogle at `http://benogle.com/2009/04/29/css-round-corners.html`.

CSS3 makes it much simpler to create rounded corners with the `border-radius` property, and the following is an example:

```
div {
    width: 100px; height: 100px;
    border-radius: 30px;
}
```

The preceding style rule will round the box corner (read the *A word on CSS Box Model* section in *Chapter 1, Responsive Web Design*) each for `30px`, as shown in the following figure:

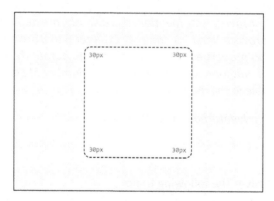

Furthermore, we can also round only to specific corners. The following code snippet, for example, will round only the top-right corner:

```
div {
    width: 100px; height: 100px;
    border-top-right-radius: 30px;
}
```

Creating drop shadow

Much the same as creating rounded corners, using images was unavoidable to create shadow effects in the website in the past. Now, adding a drop shadow has been made easy with the introduction of the box-shadow property. The box-shadow property consists of five parameters (or values):

The first parameter specifies where the shadow takes place. This parameter is optional. Set the value to inset to let the shadow appear inside the box or leave it empty to display the shadow outside.

The second parameter specifies the **shadow vertical** and **horizontal distance** from the box.

The third parameter specifies the **shadow blur** that fades the shadow; a bigger number will produce a bigger but faded shadow.

The fourth parameter specifies the **shadow expansion**; this value is slightly contradicted to the shadow blur value. This value will enlarge yet also intensify the shadow depth.

The last parameter specifies the color. The color can be in any web-compatible color format, including Hex, RGB, RGBA, and HSL.

Carrying on the preceding example, we can add up box-shadow, as follows:

```
div {
    width: 100px;
    height: 100px;
    border-radius: 30px;
    box-shadow: 5px 5px 10px 0 rgba(0,0,0,0.5);
}
```

The preceding code will output the shadow, as shown in the following figure:

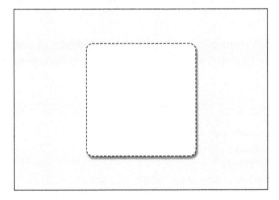

Add `inset` at the beginning if you want to show the shadow inside the box, as follows:

```
div {
    width: 100px;
    height: 100px;
    border-radius: 30px;
    box-shadow: inset 5px 5px 10px 0 rgba(0,0,0,0.5);
}
```

 The CSS3 `box-shadow` property can be applied in many creative ways, and the following is an example by Paul Underwood, for your inspiration:
`http://www.paulund.co.uk/creating-different-css3-box-shadows-effects`

CSS3 browser supports and the use of vendor prefix

Both the `border-radius` and `box-shadow` properties have been well-implemented in many browsers. Technically, if we would cater only to the latest browser versions, we do not need to include the so-called vendor prefix.

Yet, if we intend to enable these two properties, `border-radius` and `box-shadow`, back in the earliest browser versions, where they were still marked as experimental by the browser vendors such as Safari 3, Chrome 4, and Firefox 3, adding the vendor prefix is required. Each browser has its prefix as follows:

- `-webkit-`: This is the Webkit-based browsers prefix, which currently includes Safari, Chrome, and Opera.
- `-moz-`: This is the Mozilla Firefox prefix.
- `-ms-`: This is the Internet Explorer prefix. But Internet Explorer has been supporting `border-radius` and `box-shadow` since Internet Explorer 9 without the need to add this prefix.

Let's carry on our previous examples (again). With the addition of the vendor prefix to cater to the earliest versions of Chrome, Safari, and Firefox, the code would be as follows:

```
div {
    width: 100px;
    height: 100px;
    -webkit-border-radius: 30px;
    -moz-border-radius: 30px;
    border-radius: 30px;
    -webkit-box-shadow: 5px 5px 10px 0 rgba(0,0,0,0.5);
    -moz-box-shadow: 5px 5px 10px 0 rgba(0,0,0,0.5);
    box-shadow: 5px 5px 10px 0 rgba(0,0,0,0.5);
}
```

The code may turn out to be a bit longer; still it is preferable over having to cope with complicated markups and multiple style rules.

Chrome and its new browser engine, Blink

Chrome decided to fork Webkit and built its own browser engine on top of it, named Blink (http://www.chromium.org/blink). Opera, which previously discarded its initial engine (Presto) for Webkit, follows along the Chrome movement. Blink eliminates the use of the vendor prefix, so we would not find -blink- prefix or such like. In Chrome's latest versions, instead of using the vendor prefix, Chrome disables experimental features by default. Yet, we can enable it through the options in the chrome://flags page.

Customizing to placeholder text styles

With the addition of HTML5, the placeholder attribute brings the question of how to customize the placeholder text. By default, browsers display the placeholder text with a light gray color. How do we change, for example, the color or the font size?

At the time of writing this, each browser has its own way in this regard. WebKit-based browsers, such as Safari, Chrome, and Opera, use ::-webkit-input-placeholder. Internet Explorer 10 uses :-ms-input-placeholder. Firefox 4 to 18, on the other hand, use pseudo-class, :-moz-placeholder, but it has then been replaced with the pseudo-element ::-moz-placeholder (notice the double colons) since Firefox 19 to keep up with the standard.

These selectors cannot be used in tandem within a single style rule. So, the following code snippet will not work:

```
input::-webkit-input-placeholder,
input:-moz-placeholder,
input::-moz-placeholder,
input:-ms-input-placeholder {
  color: #fbb034;
}
```

They have to be declared in a single style rule declaration, as follows:

```
input::-webkit-input-placeholder {
  color: #fbb034;
}
input:-moz-placeholder {
  color: #fbb034;
}
input::-moz-placeholder {
  color: #fbb034;
```

```
}
input:-ms-input-placeholder {
  color: #fbb034;
}
```

This is definitely inefficient; we added extra lines only to achieve the same output. There isn't another viable option at the moment. The standard for styling the placeholder is still in discussion (see the CSSWG discussion at `http://wiki.csswg.org/ideas/placeholder-styling` and `http://wiki.csswg.org/spec/css4-ui#more-selectors` for more details).

Using CSS libraries

The underlying thing that distinguishes between a CSS library and a CSS framework is the problem it addresses. For example, a CSS framework, such as Blueprint (`http://www.blueprintcss.org/`), is designed as a foundation or starting point of a new website. It generally ships with various pieces of libraries to encompass many circumstances. A CSS library, on the other hand, addresses a very specific thing. Generally, a CSS library is also not tied down to a particular framework. `Animate.css` (`http://daneden.github.io/animate.css/`) and `Hover.css` (`http://ianlunn.github.io/Hover/`) are two perfect examples in this regard. Both of them are CSS libraries. They can be used along with any framework.

Herein, we will integrate two CSS libraries into the blog, namely `Normalize` (`http://necolas.github.io/normalize.css/`) and `Formalize` (`http://formalize.me/`). These CSS libraries will standardize basic element styles across different browsers and minimize styling errors that may unexpectedly occur.

Working with Koala

Once we have explored all the things that we are going to include in this project, let's set up the tool to put them together. In *Chapter 1, Responsive Web Design*, we have installed Koala. Koala is a free and open source development tool that ships with many features. In this first project, we will use Koala to compile style sheets and JavaScripts into a single file, as well as minify the codes to result in a smaller file size.

There will be about five style sheets that we are going to include in the blog. If we load all these style sheets separately, the browsers will have to pull off five HTTP requests, as shown in the following screenshot:

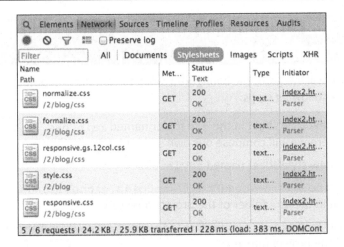

As shown in the preceding screenshot, the browser performs five HTTP requests to load all the style sheets, which have a size of 24.4 KB in total and require around 228 ms in total to load.

Combining these style sheets into a single file and squishing the codes therein will speed up the page-load performance. The style sheet can also become significantly smaller, which eventually will also save bandwidth consumption.

As shown in the following screenshot, the browser only performs one HTTP request; the style sheet size is reduced to 13.5KB, and takes only 111 ms to load. The page loads about 50 percent faster in comparison with the preceding example:

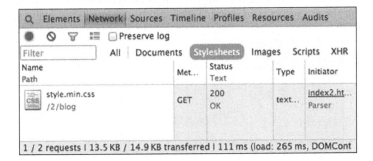

Best practices to speed up website performance:

Head over to YSlow! performance rules (`https://developer.yahoo.com/performance/rules.html`) or Google PageSpeed Insight rules (`https://developers.google.com/speed/docs/insights/rules`) for further steps to make a website load faster, aside from combining style sheets and JavaScripts.

Time for action – integrating project directory into Koala and combining the style sheets

In this section, we will integrate the configured Koala to compile and output the style sheets, by performing the following steps:

1. Create a new style sheet in the `css` folder named `main.css`. This is the prime style sheet, where we will compose our own style rules for the blog.

2. Create a new style sheet named `style.css`.

3. Download `normalize.css` (`http://necolas.github.io/normalize.css/`), and put it in the `css` folder of the project directory.

4. Download `formalize.css` (`http://formalize.me/`), and also put it in the `css` folder of the project directory.

5. Open `style.css` in Sublime Text.

6. Import the supporting style sheets using the `@import` rule in the following order, as follows:

```
@import url("css/normalize.css");
@import url("css/formalize.css");
@import url("css/responsive.gs.12col.css");
@import url("css/main.css");
@import url("css/responsive.css");
```

7. Launch Koala. Then, drag-and-drop the project directory into the Koala sidebar. Koala will show and list recognizable files, as shown in the following screenshot:

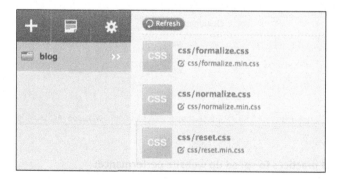

---

8. Select `style.css` and tick **Auto Compile** to compile `style.css` automatically whenever Koala detects a change in it. Have a look at the following screenshot:

9. Select the **Combine Import** option to let Koala combine the content within the style sheets (the content that was included in `style.css`) with the `@import` rule. Take a look at the following screenshot:

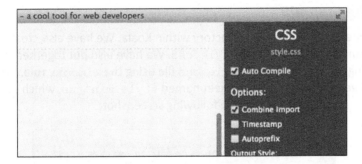

10. Set **Output Style:** to **compress**. Take a look at the following screenshot:

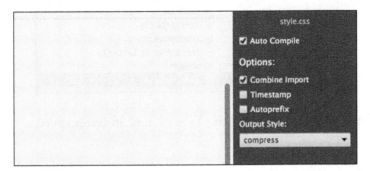

This will compress the style rules into a single line, which eventually will make the `style.css` file size smaller.

11. Click on the **Compile** button. Take a look at the following screenshot:

This will compile `style.css` and generate a new file named `style.min.css` as the output.

12. Open `index.html` and link `style.min.css.` using the following code:

```
<link href="style.min.css" rel="stylesheet">
```

What just happened?

We have just integrated the project directory within Koala. We have also created two new style sheets, namely, `main.css` and `style.css`. We have also put together five style sheets, including `main.css`, in the `style.css` file using the `@import` rule. We combined these files and generated a new style sheet named `style.min.css`, which can be found inline with `style.css`, as shown in the following screenshot:

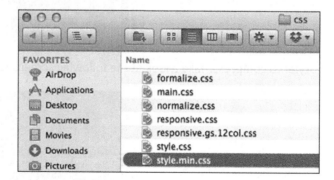

Finally, we link the minified style sheet, `style.min.css`, in `index.html`.

Have a go hero – renaming the output

The `style.min.css` name is the default name set by Koala; it inserts the suffix, `min`, to every minified output. Though it is the most popular naming convention for minified web source files, style sheets, and JavaScript, Koala allows you to rename the output to match your personal liking. To do so, click on the edit icon that is highlighted with a circle in the following screenshot:

The following are a few alternative naming ideas you can try:

- `style-min.css` (with dash)
- `styles.min.css` (with the `s`)
- `blog.css` (refers to the website name)

However, don't forget to change the name specified in the `<link>` element that refers to the style sheet as well if you decided to rename the output other than `style.min.css` as we managed in the preceding steps.

Pop quiz – website performance rules

Q1. Which of the following rules is not the one to improve website performance?

1. Minifying resources such as CSS and JavaScript.
2. Compressing image files.
3. Leveraging browser cache.
4. Using CSS shorthand properties.
5. Using CDN to deliver web resources.

Thinking mobile first

Before we get our hands on the code, let's talk about the mobile-first approach that will drive our decision on writing part of the blog style rules.

Mobile-first is one of the buzzwords in the web design community. Mobile-first is a new way of thinking on building websites of today, which also guides the pattern to build websites that are optimized for mobile use. As mentioned in *Chapter 1, Responsive Web Design*, mobile users are growing and desktop is no longer the main platform where users can access the web.

The mobile-first concept drives us to think and prioritize mobile use on building the website blocks, including how we compose style rules and media queries. In addition, adopting mobile-first thinking, as Brad Frost demonstrated in his blog post (`http://bradfrostweb.com/blog/post/7-habits-of-highly-effective-media-queries/`), allows producing leaner codes than the other way around (desktop to mobile). Herein, we will first optimize and address the blog for mobile and then enhance to the desktop version afterwards.

Mobile-first is beyond the capacity of this book. The following are some of my recommendation sources to dig into this topic further:

- Mobile First by Luke Wroblewski (`http://www.abookapart.com/products/mobile-first`)
- Mobile First Responsive Web Design by Brad Frost (`http://bradfrostweb.com/blog/web/mobile-first-responsive-web-design/`)
- Building a Better Responsive Website by Jeremy Girard (`http://www.smashingmagazine.com/2013/03/05/building-a-better-responsive-website/`)

Composing the blog styles

In the preceding sections, we added third-party styles that lay down the blog appearance fundamentals. Starting in this section, we are going to compose our own style rules for the blog. We will begin from the header then go down to the footer.

Time for action – composing the base style rules

In this section, we are going to write blog base styles. These style rules encompass the content font family, the font size, and a number of elements therein in general.

First of all, it is my personal opinion that using the default system font such as Arial and Times is so boring.

Due to the browser support and font license restriction, we were only able to use fonts that were installed in the user's operating system. Consequently, for more than a decade, we're stuck to a very limited choice of fonts we can use on the Web, and many websites use the same set of fonts, such as Arial, Times, and even Comic Sans. So, yes, these are boring fonts.

Today, with the advancement in `@font-face` specification, as well as the license of font usage on the Web, we are now able to use fonts on the website outside the font selection of the user's computer. There are also now larger collections of fonts that we can embed on the Web for free, such as the ones that we can find in Google Font (`http://www.google.com/fonts`), Open Font Library (`http://openfontlibrary.org/`), Font Squirrel (`http://www.fontsquirrel.com`), Fonts for Web (`http://fontsforweb.com/`), and Adobe Edge Web Font (`https://edgewebfonts.adobe.com/`).

I really encourage web designers to explore more the possibility of, and build, a more enriched website using the custom fonts on their websites.

Perform the following steps to compose the base style rules:

1. To make our blog look more refreshing, we will use a couple of custom fonts from the Google Font library. Google Font has made it easy for us to use fonts on the Web. Google has taken care of the hassle of writing the syntax, as well as ensuring that the font formats are compatible in all major browsers.

   Speaking of which, refer to the Paul Irish post, *Bulletproof @ font-face syntax* (`http://www.paulirish.com/2009/bulletproof-font-face-implementation-syntax/`), for further help on composing CSS3 `@font-face` syntax that works across all browsers.

2. In addition, we won't be befuddled with the font license, as Google Font is completely free. All we have to do is add a special style sheet as explained in this page `https://developers.google.com/fonts/docs/getting_started#Quick_Start`. In our case, add the following link before the prime style sheet link:

   ```
   <link href='http://fonts.googleapis.com/css?family=Droid+Serif:400
   ,700,400italic,700italic|Varela+Round' rel='stylesheet'>
   ```

Upon doing so, we will be able to use the Droid Serif font family, along with Varela Round; see these font specimens and characters in the following web pages:

- Droid Serif (`http://www.google.com/fonts/specimen/Droid+Serif`)

- Varela Round (`http://www.google.com/fonts/specimen/Varela+Round`)

3. Set the entire element box sizing to `border-box`. Add the following line (as well as the other lines in the next steps) in `main.css`:

```
* {
  -webkit-box-sizing: border-box;
  -moz-box-sizing: border-box;
  box-sizing: border-box;
  *behavior: url(/scripts/boxsizing.htc);
}
```

4. We are going to set the blog main font, that is, the font that applies to the entire content of the blog. Herein, we will use Droid Serif of Google Font. Add the following style rules after the list of `@import` style sheet:

```
body {
  font-family: "Droid Serif", Georgia, serif;
  font-size: 16px;
}
```

5. We are going to apply a different font family for the headings (`h1`, `h2`, `h3`, `h4`, `h5`, and `h6`) in order to set it apart from the body content. Herein, we will apply the second custom font family that we brought from the Google Font collection, Varela Round.

6. Add the following line to apply Varela Round to the headings:

```
h1, h2, h3, h4, h5, h6 {
  font-family: "Varela Round", Arial, sans-serif;
  font-weight: 400;
}
```

The browsers, by default, set the headings' weight to `bold` or `600`. However, Varela Round only ships with normal font weight, which equates to `400`. So, as shown in the preceding code snippet, we have also set the `font-weight` to `400` to prevent the so-called *faux-bold*.

Refer to the A List Apart article, *Say No to Faux Bold* (`http://alistapart.com/article/say-no-to-faux-bold`) for further information about faux-bold.

7. In this step, we will also customize the default anchor tag or link styles. It's my personal preference to remove the underline of the default link style.

 Even Google removes the underline of its search result (`http://www.theverge.com/2014/3/13/5503894/` `google-removes-underlined-links-site-` `redesign`).

Furthermore, we also change the link color to `#3498db`. It's blue, but subtler than the blue color applied as the default link style, as shown in the following screenshot:

8. Add the following lines to change the default link color:

```
a {
    color: #3498db;
    text-decoration: none;
}
```

9. We will set the color of the link to hover state, as well. This color appears when the mouse cursor is over the link. Herein, we set the link hover color to `#2a84bf`, the darker version of the color we set in step 4. Have a look at the following screenshot:

10. Add the following line to set the color of the link when it is in hover state, as follows:

```
a:hover {
    color: #2a84bf;
}
```

11. Make the image fluid with the following style rules, as follows:

```
img {
  max-width: 100%;
  height: auto;
}
```

In addition, these style rules will prevent the image from exceeding its container when the actual image width is larger than the container.

 Refer to A List Apart article *Fluid Images* (`http://alistapart.com/article/fluid-images`) for further detail on fluid images.

What just happened?

We have just added style rules that address some elements in the blog, namely, the headings, the link, and the image. At this stage, there isn't a significant difference yet that appears in the blog, except the font family change in the content and the headings, as well as the link color. Have a look at the following screenshot:

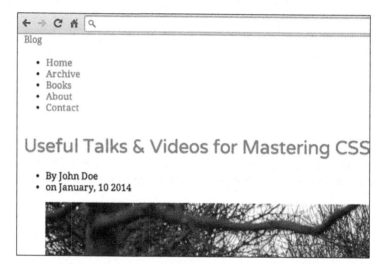

Have a go hero – customizing the link color

Please note that the link color, `#2a84bf`, is my personal selection. There are a number of considerations when choosing a color, such as the brand, the audience, and the content. The link doesn't have to be `#2a84bf`. The link color in the Starbucks website (`http://www.starbucks.co.id/about-us/pressroom`), for example, is green, which refers to its brand identity.

So, don't be afraid to explore and try new colors. The following are a few color ideas:

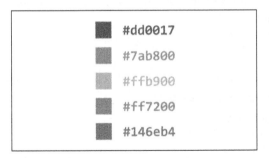

Next, we will compose the blog header and navigation style rules. The style rules will mostly be applied through the element's classes. So, before proceeding, please refer to *Chapter 2, Web Development Tools*, to see the class names and ID that we added in the elements.

Time for action – enhancing the header and the navigation appearance with CSS

The steps are as follows:

1. Open `main.css`.

2. Add some whitespace surrounding the header with `padding`, and also set the header color to `#333`, as follows:

```
.blog-header {
padding: 30px 15px;
background-color: #333;
}
```

3. To make the logo look prominent, we will set it with Varela Round font, which is the same font family we used for the headings. We also make it bigger and transform the letters all to uppercase, as follows:

```
.blog-name {
  font-family: "Varela Round", Arial, sans-serif;
  font-weight: 400;
  font-size: 42px;
  text-align: center;
  text-transform: uppercase;
}
```

4. The logo link color currently is `#2a84bf`, which is the common color we set for links `<a>`. This color does not suit well with the background color. Let's change the color to white instead, as follows:

```
.blog-name a {
    color: #fff;
}
```

5. Set the search input styles, as follows:

```
.search-form input {
  height: 36px;
  background-color: #ccc;
  color: #555;
  border: 0;
  padding: 0 10px;
  border-radius: 30px;
}
```

These style rules set the input color, border color, and the background colors. It turns the input into something as shown in the following screenshot:

6. As you can see in the preceding screenshot, the placeholder text is barely readable as the color blends with the input background color. So, let's make the text color a bit darker, as follows:

```
.search-form input::-webkit-input-placeholder {
  color: #555;
}
.search-form input:-moz-placeholder {
  color: #555;
}
.search-form input::-moz-placeholder {
  color: #555;
}
.search-form input:-ms-input-placeholder {
  color: #555;
}
```

If you use OS X or Ubuntu, you will see the glowing color that highlights the input when it is currently targeted, as shown in the following screenshot:

In OS X, the glowing color is blue. In Ubuntu, it will be orange.

7. I would like to remove this glowing effect. The glowing effect is technically shown through `box-shadow`. So, to remove this effect, we simply set the input `box-shadow` to `none`, as follows:

```
.search-form input:focus {
  -webkit-box-shadow: none;
  -moz-box-shadow: none;
  box-shadow: none;
}
```

It's worth noting that the glowing effect is part of the **User Experience** (**UX**) design, telling the users that they are currently within the input field. This UX design is particularly helpful if the users were only able to navigate the website with a keyboard.

8. So, we will have to create an effect that brings a similar UX as a replacement. Herein, we will replace the glowing effect that we removed by lightening the input background color. The following is the complete code of this step:

```
.search-form input:focus {
  -webkit-box-shadow: none;
  -moz-box-shadow: none;
  box-shadow: none;
  background-color: #bbb;
}
```

The input background color becomes lighter when it is in focus, as shown in the following screenshot:

9. We will write the style for the navigation. First, align the menu to the center, and add some whitespace at the top and the bottom of the navigation with the margin. Have a look at the following code:

```
.blog-menu {
  margin: 30px 0;
  text-align: center;
}
```

10. Remove the left-hand side padding of `<ul>`, as follows:

```
.blog-menu ul {
  padding-left: 0;
}
```

11. Add some whitespace between the menus with a margin, and remove the list bullet, as follows:

```
.blog-menu li {
  margin: 15px;
  list-style-type: none;
}
```

12. Customize the menu color and font, as follows:

```
.blog-menu a {
  color: #7f8c8d;
  font-size: 18px;
   text-transform: uppercase;
   font-family: "Varela Round", Arial, sans-serif;
}
.blog-menu a:hover {
   color: #3498db;
}
```

What just happened?

We have just decorated the header and the navigation. Corresponding to the mobile-first way of thinking, which we discussed earlier in this section, we first aim the styles to optimize the blog presentation in mobile.

Activate the Chrome mobile emulator, and you will see that the blog is optimized for a smaller screen size already; the logo and the menu, as shown in the following screenshot, are aligned to the center rather than aligned to the left:

Have a go hero – customizing the header

The blog header is given a dark color, `#333`. I truly understand that this color may look boring to some of you. Hence, freely customize the color as well as the style of the logo and the search input field. Some ideas are as follows:

- Use CSS3 gradients or image for the header background
- Replace the logo with an image through the CSS image replacement method
- Reduce the search input border radius, change the background color, and adjust the placeholder text color

Having managed the blog header as well as the navigation, we proceed to the blog content section. The content section includes the blog post items, and the blog pagination.

Time for action – enhancing the content section appearance with CSS

Perform the following steps to style the blog content:

1. Add whitespace on all sides of the content section with `padding` and `margin`, as follows

```
.blog-content {
  padding: 15px;
  margin-bottom: 30px;
}
```

2. Separate each blog post with some whitespace and borderline, as follows:

```
.post {
  margin-bottom: 60px;
  padding-bottom: 60px;
  border-bottom: 1px solid #ddd;
}
```

3. Align the title to the center, adjust the title font size a little, and change the color with the following style rules:

```
.post-title {
  font-size: 36px;
  text-align: center;
  margin-top: 0;
}
.post-title a {
  color: #333;
}
.post-title a:hover {
  color: #3498db;
}
```

4. Below the title, we have `post-meta`, which consists of the post author name and the post publishing date. Similar to the title, we also adjust the font size and the whitespace, and change the font color, as follows:

```
.post-meta {
  font-size: 18px;
  margin: 20px 0 0;
  text-align: center;
  color: #999;
}
.post-meta ul {
  list-style-type: none;
  padding-left: 0;
}
.post-meta li {
  margin-bottom: 10px;
}
```

5. The post thumbnail, as you can see in the following screenshot, looks small and squished due to the margin on all its sides:

6. Let's remove these margins, as follows:

```
.post-thumbnail {
  margin: 0;
}
```

Some of the images, as shown in the following screenshot, have a caption:

7. Let's style it to make it look distinctive from the rest of the content and also show that it is an image caption. Add the following lines of code to style the caption:

```
.post-thumbnail figcaption {
  color: #bdc3c7;
  margin-top: 15px;
  font-size: 16px;
  font-style: italic;
}
```

8. Adjust the post excerpt font size, color, and line height, as follows:

```
.post-excerpt {
  color: #555;
  font-size: 18px;
  line-height: 30px;
}
```

9. Starting in this step, we will write the style of the blog pagination. First, let's make some adjustments to the font size, the font family, the whitespace, the position, and the alignment, as shown in the following code:

```
.blog-pagination {
  text-align: center;
  font-size: 16px;
  position: relative;
  margin: 60px 0;
}
.blog-pagination ul {
  padding-left: 0;
}
.blog-pagination li,
.blog-pagination a {
  display: block;
  width: 100%;
}
.blog-pagination li {
  font-family: "Varela Round", Arial, sans-serif;
  color: #bdc3c7;
  text-transform: uppercase;
  margin-bottom: 10px;
}
```

10. Decorate the pagination link with rounded corner borders, as follows:

```
.blog-pagination a {
  -webkit-border-radius: 30px;
  -moz-border-radius: 30px;
  border-radius: 30px;
  color: #7f8c8d;
  padding: 15px 30px;
  border: 1px solid #bdc3c7;
}
```

11. Specify the link decoration when the mouse cursor hovers over the links, as follows:

```
.blog-pagination a:hover {
  color: #fff;
  background-color: #7f8c8d;
  border: 1px solid #7f8c8d;
}
```

12. Finally, place the page number indicator at the top of the pagination links with the following style rules:

```
.blog-pagination .pageof {
  position: absolute;
  top: -30px;
}
```

What just happened?

We just styled the blog content section—including the page navigation (pagination), and the following screenshot shows how the content section looks:

Have a go hero – improving the content section

Most of the style rules we applied in the content section are decorative. It's something that you don't have to follow forcefully. Feel free to improve the styles to follow your personal taste.

You can perform the following modifications:

◆ Customize the post title font family and the colors

◆ Apply border colors or rounded corners for the post image

◆ Change the pagination border colors, or make the background more colorful

Next, we will style the footer, the last section of the blog.

Time for action – enhancing the footer section appearance with CSS

Perform the following steps to enhance the footer style:

1. Adjust the footer font, color, and the margin, as follows:

```
.blog-footer {
  background-color: #ecf0f1;
  padding: 60px 0;
  font-family: "Varela Round", Arial, sans-serif;
  margin-top: 60px;
}
.blog-footer,
.blog-footer a {
  color: #7f8c8d;
}
```

2. The footer contains social media links. Let's adjust the styles that encompass the margin, padding, alignment, colors, and whitespace, as follows:

```
.social-media {
  margin: 0 0 30px;
}
.social-media ul {
  margin: 0;
  padding-left: 0;
}
.social-media li {
  margin: 0 8px 10px;
  list-style: none;
}
.social-media li,
```

```
.social-media a {
  font-size: 18px;
}
.social-media a:hover {
  color: #333;
}
```

3. Set the margin-top out of the copyright container.

```
.copyright {
  margin-top: 0;
}
```

4. Align the footer content to the center, as follows:

```
.social-media,
.copyright {
  text-align: center;
}
```

What just happened?

We have just styled the footer section, and the following screenshot shows how the blog footer will look:

Optimize the blog for desktop

The blog is currently optimized for mobile, or narrow viewport size. If you view it in a larger viewport size, you will find that some elements are misplaced or are not properly aligned. The blog logo and the navigation, for example, are currently aligned to the center, as you can see in the following screenshot:

As per our blueprint that we have shown you in *Chapter 3, Constructing a Simple Responsive Blog with Responsive.gs*, the logo should align to the left-hand side and each menu link should be displayed inline. In the upcoming steps, we will fix these through Media Queries; we will optimize the blog for desktop view.

Time for action – composing style rules for desktop

Perform the following steps to compose style rules for desktop:

1. Open `responsive.css` in Sublime Text.

2. Add the following media query:

```
@media screen and (min-width: 640px) {
  // add style rules here
}
```

We will add all the style rules in the following steps within this media query. This media query specification will apply the style rules within the viewport width starting from 640 px and up.

1. Align the blog logo to the left-hand side, as follows:

```css
.blog-name {
  text-align: left;
  margin-bottom: 0;
}
```

2. Display the list item of the navigation menu, post meta, and social media inline, as follows:

```css
.blog-menu li,
.post-meta li,
.social-media li {
      display: inline;
}
```

3. Increase the post title size, as follows:

```css
.post-title {
  font-size: 48px;
}
```

4. Also, display the blog pagination links inline, as follows:

```css
.blog-pagination li,
.blog-pagination a {
  display: inline;
}
```

5. Put the pagination page indicator in its initial position—inline with the blog pagination link, as follows:

```css
.blog-pagination .pageof {
  position: relative;
  top: 0;
  padding: 0 20px;
}
```

6. Align the social media links in the footer to the left and the copyright notice to the right, as follows:

```css
.social-media {
  text-align: left;
}
.copyright {
  text-align: right;
}
```

What just happened?

We have just added style rules that address the blog for the desktop view. If you are now viewing the blog in the viewport width that is larger than 640 px, you should find that the elements in the blog such as the logo and the navigation menu are in their common position, as shown in the following screenshot:

Making Internet Explorer more capable with polyfills

With the use of glorious CSS3 and HTML5 features, comes a consequence: the layout failed and is broken in the old Internet Explorer, as you can see in the following screenshot:

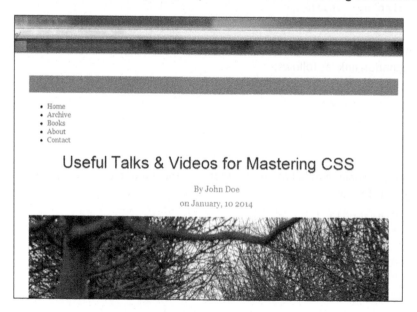

If you are okay with it, you can skip this section and head over to the next project immediately. However, if you feel adventurous, let's proceed to this section and fix those bugs.

Time for action – patch Internet Explorer with polyfills

Perform the steps to patch Internet Explorer with polyfills:

1. We have a number of polyfills in the scripts folder namely `html5shiv.js`, `respond.js`, and `placeholder.js`. Let's combine these scripts into a single file.

2. First, create a new JavaScript file named `polyfills.js` that will hold the content of those polyfill scripts.

3. Open `polyfills.js` in Sublime Text.

4. Add the following lines to import the polyfill scripts:

```
// @koala-prepend "html5shiv.js"
// @koala-prepend "respond.js"
// @koala-prepend "placeholder.js"
```

> The `@koala-prepend` directive is the Koala proprietary directive to import JavaScript files. Read more about it in the Koala documentation page at `https://github.com/oklai/koala/wiki/JS-CSS-minify-and-combine`.

5. In Koala, select `polyfills.js`, and click on the **Compile** button, as shown in the following screenshot:

By this step, Koala will have generated the minified file named `polyfills.min.js`.

6. Open `index.html`, and link `polyfills.js` before `</head>`, as follows:

```
<!--[if lt IE 9]>
<script type="text/javascript" src="scripts/polyfills.min.js"></
script>
<![endif]-->
```

> Since this script is only needed in Internet Explorer 8 and below, we encapsulate them with the Internet Explorer Conditional Comment, `<!--[if lt IE 9]>`, as you can see in the preceding code snippet.
>
> Refer to the QuirksMode article for further information about Internet Explorer Conditional Comments at `http://www.quirksmode.org/css/condcom.html`.

What just happened?

We just applied polyfills in the blog to patch Internet Explorer rendering issues with HTML5 and Media Queries. These polyfills work out-of-the-box. Refresh Internet Explorer, and voila! Have a look at the following screenshot:

The style rules are applied, the layout is in position, and the placeholder text is there.

Have a go hero – polish the blog for Internet Explorer

We will end this project. But, as you can see from the preceding screenshot, there are still many things to address to make the blog appearance in the old Internet Explorer as good as in the latest browsers. For example:

◆ Referring to the preceding screenshot, the placeholder text is currently aligned to the top. You can fix it and make it align vertically to the center.

◆ You can also apply a polyfill named CSS3Pie (`http://css3pie.com/`) that brings the CSS3 border radius in Internet Explorer to make the search input field rounded as it is in the latest browser versions.

Summary

We completed the first project; we have built a simple, responsive blog using Responsive. gs. The end result of the blog may not be that enticing for you. It is also far from polished, particularly in the old Internet Explorer; as mentioned, there are still many things to address in that regard. Still, I hope you can take something useful from the process, the techniques, and the codes therein.

To summarize, here is what we have done in this chapter, enhanced and polished the blog with CSS3, used Koala to combine and minimize style sheets and JavaScript files, and applied polyfills to patch Internet Explorer issues with HTML5 and CSS3.

In the next chapter, we will start the second project. We are going to explore another framework to build a more extensive and responsive website.

5
Developing a Portfolio Website with Bootstrap

Bootstrap (`http://getbootstrap.com/`) is one of the sturdiest frontend development frameworks. It ships with amazing features, such as a responsive grid, user interface components, and JavaScript libraries that let us build responsive websites up and running quickly.

Bootstrap is so popular that the web development community positively supports it by developing extensions in a variety of forms to add extra features. In case the standard features that come with Bootstrap are not sufficient, there can be an extension to cover your particular requirements.

In this chapter, we will start our second project. We will employ Bootstrap to build a responsive portfolio website. So, this chapter apparently would be useful for those who work in creative fields such as photography, graphic design, and illustrating.

Herein, we will also employ a Bootstrap extension to empower the portfolio website with off-canvas navigation. Following Bootstrap, we will turn to LESS as the foundation of the website style sheets.

Let's move on.

The discussion that we are going to cover in this chapter will include the following topics:

- ◆ Explore Bootstrap components
- ◆ Look into the Bootstrap extension to bring off-canvas navigation

- Examine the portfolio website blueprint and design
- Set up and organize the project directories and assets with Bower and Koala
- Construct the portfolio website HTML structure

The Bootstrap components

Unlike the Responsive.gs framework that we used in the first project, Bootstrap is shipped with extra components, which are commonly used in the Web. Hence, before we step further into developing the portfolio website, first let's explore these components, mainly those of which we will employ within the website, such as the responsive grid, the buttons, and the form elements.

 Frankly, the official Bootstrap website (http://getbootstrap.com/) is always the best source to be up-to-date with anything related to Bootstrap. So, herein, I would like to point out the key things that are straightforward.

The Bootstrap responsive grid

Bootstrap comes with a Responsive Grid System, along with the supporting classes that form the columns and the rows. In Bootstrap, we build the column using these prefix classes: col-xs-, col-sm-, col-md-, and col-lg-. This is then followed by the column number, ranging from 1 to 12, to define the column size as well as to aim the column for a specific viewport size. See the following table for more detail on the prefixes:

Prefix	Description
col-xs-	This specifies the column for the Bootstrap-defined smallest (extra small) viewport size, which is equal to or less than 768 px
col-sm-	This specifies the column for the Bootstrap-defined small viewport size, which is equal to or greater than 768 px.
col-md-	This specifies the column for the Bootstrap-defined medium viewport size, which is equal to or greater than 992 px
col-lg-	This specifies the column for the Bootstrap-defined large viewport size, which is equal to or greater than 1,200 px

In the following example, we set out three columns in a row, with each column assigned a col-sm-4 class:

```
<div class="row">
  <div class="col-sm-4"></div>
  <div class="col-sm-4"></div>
  <div class="col-sm-4"></div>
</div>
```

So, each column will have the same size, and they will scale down up to the Bootstrap-defined small viewport size (≥ 768px). The following screenshot shows how the preceding markup turns out in the browser (by adding a few styles):

View the example in the viewport size, which is smaller than 768 px, and all these columns will start to stack up—the first column at the top and the third column at the very bottom, as shown in the following screenshot:

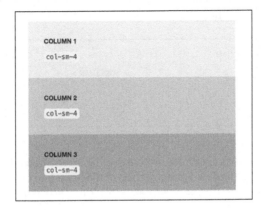

Furthermore, we can add multiple classes to specify the column proportion within multiple viewport sizes, as follows:

```
<div class="row">
    <div class="col-sm-6 col-md-2 col-lg-4"></div>
    <div class="col-sm-3 col-md-4 col-lg-4"></div>
    <div class="col-sm-3 col-md-6 col-lg-4"></div>
</div>
```

Given the preceding example, the columns will have the same size within the Bootstrap-defined large viewport size (≥ 1,200 px), as shown in the following screenshot:

The column proportion then starts to shift when we view it in the medium viewport size following the assigned classes on each column. The first column width will become smaller, the second column will retain the same proportion, while the third column will be larger, as shown in the following screenshot:

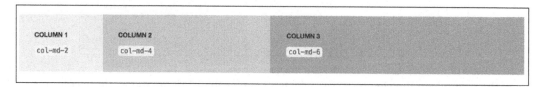

The column proportion will start to shift again when the website is at the threshold of the Bootstrap-defined medium- and small-viewport size, which is approximately at 991px, as shown in the following screenshot:

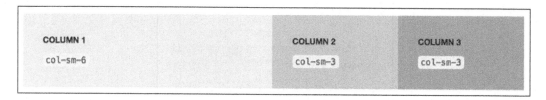

For further assistance on constructing a Bootstrap grid, head over to the Grid System section of the Bootstrap official website (http://getbootstrap.com/css/#grid).

Bootstrap buttons and forms

Other components that we will incorporate into the website are buttons and forms. We will create an online contact through which users will be able get in touch. In Bootstrap, the button is formed with the `btn` class followed by `btn-default` to apply Bootstrap default styles, as shown in the following code:

```
<button type="button" class="btn btn-default">Submit</button>
<a class="btn btn-default">Send</a>
```

Replace the `btn-default` class with `btn-primary`, `btn-success`, or `btn-info` to give the buttons the colors specified, as shown in the following code:

```
<button type="button" class="btn btn-info">Submit</button>
<a class="btn btn-success">Send</a>
```

The code snippet defines the button size with these classes: `btn-lg` to make the button large, `btn-sm` to make it small, and `btn-xs` to make the button even smaller, as shown in the following code:

```
<button type="button" class="btn btn-info btn-lg">Submit</button>
<a class="btn btn-success btn-sm">Send</a>
```

The following screenshot shows how the button-size changes with the look, when the preceding classes are added:

Bootstrap allows us to display buttons in a number of ways, such as displaying a series of buttons inline together or adding a dropdown toggle in a button. For further assistance and details on constructing these types of buttons, head over to the button groups (`http://getbootstrap.com/components/#btn-groups`) and the button dropdown (`http://getbootstrap.com/components/#btn-dropdowns`) sections of Bootstrap's official website.

The Bootstrap buttons groups and buttons with a dropdown toggle

Bootstrap also provided a handful of reusable classes to style the form elements, such as `<input>` and `<textarea>`. To style the form elements, Bootstrap uses the `form-control` class. The style is light and decent, as shown in the following screenshot:

For more information regarding styling and arranging the form element in Bootstrap, refer to the form section of the Bootstrap official page (`http://getbootstrap.com/css/#forms`).

Bootstrap Jumbotron

Bootstrap describes Jumbotron as follows:

> *"A lightweight, flexible component that can optionally extend the entire viewport to showcase key content on your site" (http://getbootstrap.com/components/#jumbotron)*

Jumbotron is a special section to display the website's first-line message, such as the marketing copy, catchphrases, or special offers, and additionally a button. Jumbotron is typically placed above the fold and below the navigation bar. To construct a Jumbotron section in Bootstrap, apply the `jumbotron` class, as follows:

```
<div class="jumbotron">
   <h1>Hi, This is Jumbotron</h1>
<p>Place the marketing copy, catchphrases, or special offerings.</p>
   <p><a class="btn btn-primary btn-lg" role="button">Got it!</a></p>
</div>
```

With the Bootstrap default styles, the following is how the Jumbotron looks:

This is the Jumbotron appearance with the default style

 Further details about Bootstrap Jumbotron can be found in the Bootstrap components page at `http://getbootstrap.com/components/#jumbotron`.

Bootstrap third-party extensions

It's impossible to cater to everyone's needs, and the same thing applies to Bootstrap as well. A number of extensions are created in many forms—from CSS, JavaScript, icons, starter templates, and themes—to extend Bootstrap. Find the full list on this page (`http://bootsnipp.com/resources`).

In this project, we will include an extension named Jasny Bootstrap (`http://jasny.github.io/bootstrap/`), developed by Arnold Daniels. We will use it primarily to incorporate off-canvas navigation. The off-canvas navigation is a popular pattern in responsive design; the menu navigation will first set off the visible area of the website and will only slide-in typically by clicking or tapping, as illustrated in the following screenshot:

The off-canvas section slide-in when users click on the three-stripe icon

Jasny Bootstrap off-canvas

Jasny Bootstrap is an extension that adds extra building blocks to the original Bootstrap. Jasny Bootstrap is designed with Bootstrap in mind; it follows Bootstrap conventions in almost every aspect of it, including the HTML markups, the class naming, and the JavaScript functions as well as the APIs.

As mentioned, we will use this extension to include off-canvas navigation in the portfolio website. The following is an example code snippet to construct off-canvas navigation with Jasny Bootstrap:

```
<nav id="offcanvas-nav" class="navmenu navmenu-default navmenu-fixed-
left offcanvas" role="navigation">
  <ul class="nav navmenu-nav">
    <li class="active"><a href="#">Home</a></li>
    <li><a href="#">Link</a></li>
    <li><a href="#">Link</a></li>
  </ul>
</nav>
```

```
<div class="navbar navbar-default navbar-fixed-top">
<button type="button" class="navbar-toggle" data-toggle="offcanvas"
data-target="#offcanvas-nav" data-target="body">
    <span class="icon-bar"></span>
    <span class="icon-bar"></span>
    <span class="icon-bar"></span>
  </button>
</div>
```

As you can see from the preceding code snippet, constructing off-canvas navigation requires a bunch of HTML elements, classes, and attributes in the mix. To begin with, we need two elements, `<nav>` and `<div>`, to contain respectively the menu and the button to toggle the navigation menu on and off. The `<nav>` element is given an ID as a unique reference of which menu to target via the `data-target` attribute in `<button>`.

A handful of classes and attributes are added within these elements to specify the colors, backgrounds, position, and functions:

♦ `navmenu`: Jasny Bootstrap has a new type of navigation, called navmenu. The `navmenu` class will display the navigation vertically, and placed on the side—right-hand or left-hand—of the website content, instead of at the top.

♦ `navmenu-default`: The class that will set the `navmenu` class with the default styles, which is dominated by light gray. Use the `navmenu-inverse` class instead if you prefer a dark color. Have a look at the following screenshot:

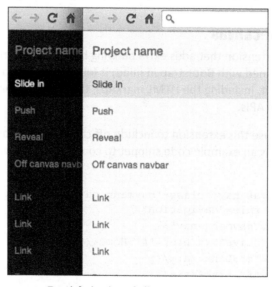

Two default colors of off-canvas navigation

- The `navmenu-fixed-left` class positions the navmenu on the left-hand side. Use the `navmenu-fixed-right` class to set it on the right-hand side instead.

- The `offcanvas` class is the prime class to set the navigation menu off the canvas.

- The `data-target="#offcanvas-nav"` code in `<button>` acts as a selector that refers to a specific navigation menu with the given ID.

- The `data-toggle="offcanvas"` code tells the button to toggle the off-canvas navigation. In addition, the original Bootstrap ships with several types of `data-toggle` to hook up different widgets, such as the modal (`data-toggle="modal"`), dropdown (`data-toggle="dropdown"`), and tab (`data-toggle="tab"`).

- The data-target="body" lets the website body slide along with the off-canvas navigation at the same time when being toggled on and off. Jasny Bootstrap calls it as push menu; follow this page (`http://jasny.github.io/bootstrap/examples/navmenu-push/`) to see it in action.

 In addition, Jasny Bootstrap provides two extra types of off-canvas navigation, named slide-in menu (`http://jasny.github.io/bootstrap/examples/navmenu/`) and reveal menu (`http://jasny.github.io/bootstrap/examples/navmenu-reveal/`)—follow the inclusive URL to see them in action.

Digging into Bootstrap

Exploring every inch of Bootstrap component is beyond the capacity of this book. Hence, we only discussed a couple of things from Bootstrap that will be essential to the project. Aside from the Bootstrap official website (`http://getbootstrap.com/`), the following are a couple of dedicated references that dig deep into Bootstrap that you can look into:

- Bootstrap tutorials for beginners by Coder's Guide (`http://www.youtube.com/watch?v=YXVoqJEwqoQ`), a series of video tutorials that help beginners to get up and running with Bootstrap

- *Twitter Bootstrap Web Development How-To, David Cochran, Packt Publishing* (`http://www.packtpub.com/web-development/twitter-bootstrap-web-development-how-instant`)

- *Mobile First Bootstrap, Alexandre Magno, Packt Publishing* (`http://www.packtpub.com/web-development/mobile-first-bootstrap`)

Using font icons

Retina or **high-definition (HD)** display makes everything on the screen look sharper and more vibrant. But, the problem lies with the legacy images or web icons brought before the advent of HD display. These images typically are served as a bitmap or a raster image, and they turn blurry on this screen, as shown in the following screenshot:

A series of icons that blur on the edges, as displayed in retina display

We do not want that to happen in our website, so we will have to use a font icon that is more scalable and stays sharp in a high-definition screen.

To tell the truth, Bootstrap ships with a font icon set called Glyphicon. Sadly, it does not come with the social media icons that we need. After going through a number of font-icon sets, I finally opted for Ionicons (`http://ionicons.com/`). Herein, we will use the alternative version that comes with LESS, which is developed by Lance Hudson (`https://github.com/lancehudson/ionicons-less`), so we will be able to integrate with Bootstrap seamlessly, which also happens to use LESS.

Examining the portfolio website layout

Before we start building the blocks and edges of the website, let's take a look the website wireframe. This wireframe will be the reference and give us the picture of how the website layout will be organized both in the mobile and desktop view.

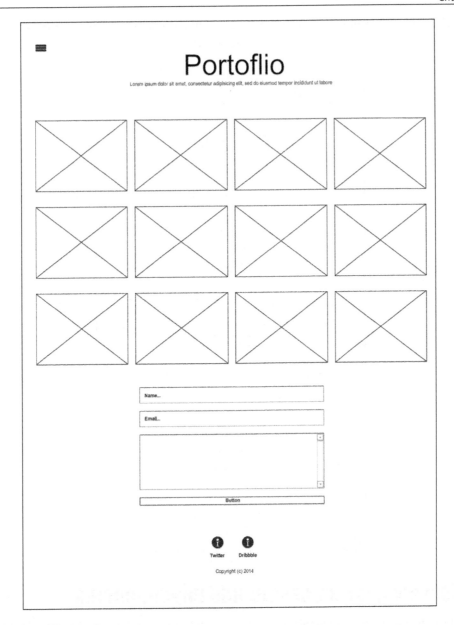

The preceding screenshot shows the website layout for the desktop or—technically—the wide viewport size.

The website will have a button positioned at the top-left of the website with a so-called **hamburger** icon to slide in the off-canvas menu. Then comes the website's first line, which says the website name and a line of catchphrase. The subsequent section will contain the portfolio images, while the last section will contain an online form and social media icons.

The mobile view looks more simplified, yet maintaining the same logical structure as in the desktop view layout, as shown in the following screenshot:

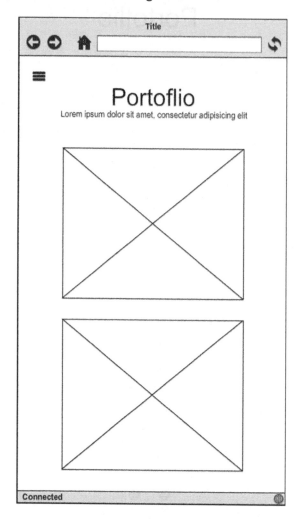

Project directories, assets, and dependencies

Let's start off the project by organizing the project directories and assets that include the dependencies, images, and font icon.

 What is dependency? Dependency herein is a file or a package of files, such as CSS and JavaScript library, that is needed to run the project and build the website.

In this project, we will put Bower (`http://bower.io/`) into practice to organize the project dependencies. Bower, as we briefly mentioned in *Chapter 1, Responsive Web Design*, is a frontend package manager that streamlines the way to install, remove, and update frontend development libraries, such as jQuery, Normalize, and HTML5Shiv.

Time for action – organizing project directories, assets, and installing project dependencies with Bower

In this section, we are going to add the project dependencies that include the Bootstrap, Jasny Bootstrap, Ionicons, and HTML5Shiv. We will install them using Bower so that we are able to maintain them—remove and update them—more seamlessly in the future.

In addition, since this might be the first time for many of you using Bower, I will walk you through the process at a slow pace, bit by bit. Please perform the following steps thoroughly:

1. In the `htdocs` folder, create a new folder, and name it `portfolio`. This is the project directory, where we will add all project files and folders to.

2. In the `portfolio` folder, create a new folder named `assets`. We will put the project assets, such as image, JavaScript, and style sheet in this folder.

3. In the assets folder, create these following folders:

    ❑ `img` to contain the website images and image-based icons

    ❑ `js` to contain the JavaScript files

    ❑ `fonts` to contain the font icon set

    ❑ `less` to contain the LESS style sheets

    ❑ `css` as the output folder of LESS

4. Create `index.html` as the website's main page.

5. Add the images for the website in the `img` folder; this includes the portfolio images and the icons for a mobile device, as shown in the following screenshot:

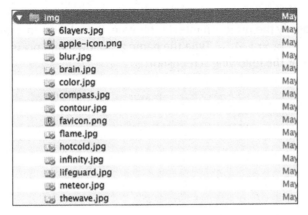

This website has around 14 images including the icons for mobile devices. I would like to thank my friend Yoga Perdana (https://dribbble.com/yoga) for allowing me to use his wonderful work in this book. You can find these images bundled along with this book. But, certainly, you can replace them with your very own images.

6. We will install the dependencies—packages, libraries, JavaScript, or CSS that are required to run the project, as well as to build the website—through Bower. But, before running any Bower command to install the dependencies, we would like to set the project as a Bower project using the `bower init` command to define the project specification in `bower.json`, such as the project name, the version, and the author.

7. To begin with, open a terminal or command prompt if you are using Windows. Then, navigate to the project directory using the `cd` command, as follows:

   ❑ In Windows: `cd \xampp\htdocs\portfolio`

   ❑ In OS X: `cd /Applications/XAMPP/htdocs/portfolio`

   ❑ In Ubuntu: `cd /opt/lampp/htdocs/portfolio`

8. Type `bower init`, as shown in the following screenshot:

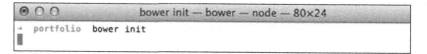

This command, `bower init`, initiates our project as a Bower project. This command also leads to a number of prompts to fill to describe the project such as the project name, the project version, the author, and so on.

9. First, we specify the project name. In this case, I would like to name the project `responsive-portfolio`. Type the name as follows, and press *Enter* to proceed. Have a look at the following screenshot:

10. Specify the project version. Since the project is new, let's simply set it to `1.0.0`, as shown in the following screenshot:

```
● ○ ○                bower init — bower — node — 80×24
↪   portfolio  bower init
? name: responsive-portfolio
? version: (0.0.0) 1.0.0▊
```

11. Press *Enter* to proceed.

12. Specify the project description. This prompt is entirely optional. You may leave it empty if you think it's not required for your project. In this case, I will describe the project as `a responsive portfolio website built with Bootstrap`, as shown in the following screenshot:

```
● ○ ○                bower init — bower — node — 80×24
↪   portfolio  bower init
? name: responsive-portfolio
? version: 1.0.0
? description: a responsive portfolio website buildt with Bootstrap▊
```

13. Specify the main file of the project. This certainly will vary depending on the project. Herein, let's set the main file to `index.html`, the website's home page, as shown in the following screenshot:

```
● ○ ○                bower init — bower — node — 80×24
↪   portfolio  bower init
? name: responsive-portfolio
? version: 1.0.0
? description: a responsive portfolio website buildt with Bootstrap
? main file: index.html▊
```

14. This prompts the question, "what types of modules does this package expose?" It specifies what the package is used for. In this case, simply select the global option, as shown in the following screenshot:

```
● ○ ○                bower init — bower — node — 80×24
↪   portfolio  bower init
? name: responsive-portfolio
? version: 1.0.0
? description: a responsive portfolio website buildt with Bootstrap
? main file: index.html
? what types of modules does this package expose?:
  o amd
  o es6
)⊗ globals
  o node
  o yui
```

15. Press the Space Bar key to select it, and press *Enter* to continue.

> This prompt describes what the module technology in the project (our project) is meant for. Our project is not attached to a particular technology or module; it's just a plain static website with HTML, CSS, and a few lines of JavaScript. We are not building Node, YUI, or AMD modules. Thus, it is best to select the `globals` option.

16. The **keywords** prompt tells the project relation. In this case, I would like to fill it as `portfolio, responsive, bootstrap`, as shown in the following screenshot. Press *Enter* to continue:

```
● ○ ○                    bower init — bower — node — 80×24
→  portfolio   bower init
? name: responsive-portfolio
? version: 1.0.0
? description: a responsive portfolio website buildt with Bootstrap
? main file: index.html
? what types of modules does this package expose?: globals
? keywords: portfolio, responsive, bootstrap
```

The **keywords** prompt is optional. You can leave it empty if you want by pressing the *Enter* key with the value left empty.

17. The **authors** prompt specifies the author of the project. This prompt is prepopulated with your computer user name and e-mail that you have registered in the system. Yet, you can overwrite it by specifying a new name and pressing *Enter* to continue, as shown in the following screenshot:

```
● ○ ○                    bower init — bower — node — 80×24
→  portfolio   bower init
? name: responsive-portfolio
? version: 1.0.0
? description: a responsive portfolio website buildt with Bootstrap
? main file: index.html
? what types of modules does this package expose?: globals
? keywords: portfolio, responsive, bootstrap
? authors: (Thoriq Firdaus <tfirdaus@creatiface.com>)
```

> If the project has multiple authors, you can specify each author with a comma separator, as follows:
>
> **authors:** John Doe, Jane Doe.

18. Specify the project license. Herein, we will simply set it to the `MIT` license. The `MIT` license grants anyone to do whatever he or she wants with the code in the project, including modification, sublicensing, and commercial use. Have a look at the following screenshot:

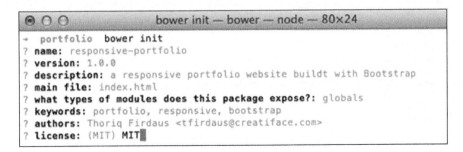

 Refer to Choose A License (`http://choosealicense.com/`) to find other types of licenses.

19. Specify the home page of the project. This could be your own website repository. In this case, I would like to set it with my personal domain, `creatiface.com`, as shown in the following screenshot:

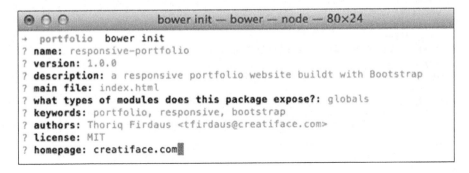

20. In the **set currently installed components as dependencies?:** command, type n (no), as we haven't installed any dependencies or packages yet, as shown in the following screenshot:

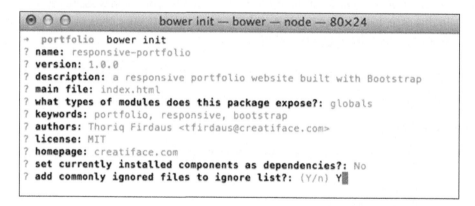

21. The **Add commonly ignored files to ignore list?** command will create the .gitignore file containing a list of common files to exclude from the Git repository. Type Y for yes. Have a look at the following screenshot:

I will use Git to manage the code revision and will upload it to a Git repository, such as Github or Bitbucket, hence I selected Y (yes). If, however, you are not familiar with Git yet, and do not plan to host the project in a Git repository, you may ignore this prompt and type n. Git is beyond the scope of this book's discussion. To learn more about Git, the following is the best reference I recommend:

Learn Git for beginners by GitTower (http://www.git-tower.com/learn/).

22. For the **would you like to mark this package as private which prevents it from being accidentally published to the registry?** command type Y as we won't register our project to the Bower registry. Have a look at the following screenshot:

```
● ○ ○                   bower init — bower — node — 80×24
→   portfolio   bower init
?  name: responsive-portfolio
?  version: 1.0.0
?  description: a responsive portfolio website built with Bootstrap
?  main file: index.html
?  what types of modules does this package expose?: globals
?  keywords: portfolio, responsive, bootstrap
?  authors: Thoriq Firdaus <tfirdaus@creatiface.com>
?  license: MIT
?  homepage: creatiface.com
?  set currently installed components as dependencies?: No
?  add commonly ignored files to ignore list?: Yes
?  would you like to mark this package as private which prevents it from
cidentally published to the registry?: (y/N) Y
```

23. Examine the output. If it looks good, type Y to generate the output within the bower.json file, as shown in the following screenshot:

```
● ○ ○                   bower init — bower — node — 80×24
  ],
  description: 'a responsive portfolio website built with Bootstrap',
  main: 'index.html',
  moduleType: [
    'globals'
  ],
  keywords: [
    'portfolio',
    'responsive',
    'bootstrap'
  ],
  license: 'MIT',
  homepage: 'creatiface.com',
  private: true,
  ignore: [
    '**/.*',
    'node_modules',
    'bower_components',
    'test',
    'tests'
  ]
}

?  Looks good?: (Y/n)
```

24. There are a number of libraries we want to install. To begin with, let's install Bootstrap with the `bower install bootstrap --save` command, as shown in the following screenshot:

```
● ○ ○
→  portfolio   bower install bootstrap --save
```

The `--save` parameter following the command will register Bootstrap as the project dependency in `bower.json`. If you open it, you should find it recorded under the dependencies, as shown in the following screenshot:

```
21        "**/.*",
22        "node_modules",
23        "bower_components",
24        "test",
25        "tests"
26      ],
27      "dependencies": {
28        "bootstrap": "3.1.1"
29      }
30    }
31
```

You should also find the Bootstrap package saved in a new folder, `bower_components`, along with jQuery, which is a Bootstrap dependency, as shown in the following screenshot:

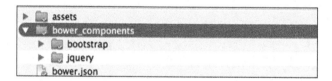

```
▶  📁  assets
▼  📁  bower_components
   ▶  📁  bootstrap
   ▶  📁  jquery
      📄  bower.json
```

25. Install the Bootstrap extension, Jasny Bootstrap, with the `bower install jasny-bootstrap -save` command.

26. Install Ionicons with the LESS style sheet, with the `bower install ionicons-less -save` command.

27. The Ionicons package ships with the font files. Move them to the `fonts` folder of the project directory, as shown in the following screenshot:

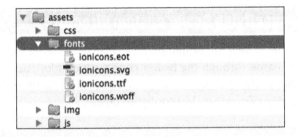

28. Finally, install HTML5Shiv to enable the new elements of HTML5 in Internet Explorer 8 and below, with the `bower install html5shiv --save` command.

What just happened?

We just created folders and the website home page document, `index.html`. Images and icons that are going to be displayed on the website are also prepared. We also recorded the project specification in `bower.json`. Through this file, we can tell that the project is named `responsive-portfolio`, currently at version 1.0.0, and has a couple of dependencies, as follows:

- Bootstrap (`https://github.com/twbs/bootstrap`)
- Jasny Bootstrap (`http://jasny.github.io/bootstrap/`)
- Ionicons with LESS (`https://github.com/lancehudson/ionicons-less`)
- HTML5Shiv (`https://github.com/aFarkas/html5shiv`)

We have downloaded these libraries via the `bower install` command, which is leaner than having to download and extract the `.zip` package. All the libraries should have been added within a folder named `bower_components`, as shown in the following screenshot:

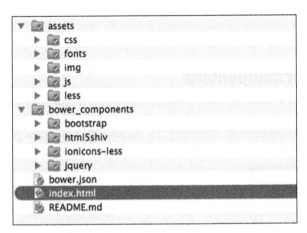

Have a go hero – specifying Bower custom directory

Bower, by default, creates a new folder named `bower_components`. Bower allows us to configure the folder name through the Bower configuration file, `.bowerrc`. Change the folder name as per your preference by creating `.bowerrc`. Follow this reference (`http://bower.io/docs/config/`) to configure bower.

Pop quiz – test your understanding on Bower commands

Q1. We have shown you how to install and update libraries with Bower. The question now is: how to remove the library that has been installed?

1. Run the `bower remove` command.
2. Run the `bower uninstall` command.
3. Run the `bower delete` command.

Q2. Besides installing and removing the library, we can also search the availability of the library in the Bower registry. How to search a library through the Bower registry?

1. Run `bower search` followed by a keyword.
2. Run `bower search` followed by the library name.
3. Run `bower browse` followed by a keyword.

Q3. Bower also allows us to look into the detail of the package properties, such as the package version, dependencies, author, etc. What command do we perform to look into these details?

1. `bower info.`
2. `bower detail.`
3. `bower property.`

Updating Bower components

As the dependencies are installed with Bower, maintaining the project will be more streamlined. These libraries can be updated to the newer version at a later time. With the use of Bower commands, updating the libraries that we have just installed is practically leaner than downloading the `.zip` package and manually moving the files into the project directory.

Run the `bower list` command to see all installed Bower packages, and check whether a new version of the packages is available, as shown in the following screenshot:

```
○ ○ ○
→ portfolio  bower list
bower check-new      Checking for new versions of the project dependencie
responsive-portfolio#1.0.0
├── bootstrap#3.1.1 (latest is 3.2.0)
│   └── jquery#2.1.1
├── html5shiv#3.7.2
├── ionicons-less#1.4.1
├── jasny-bootstrap#3.1.3
│   ├── bootstrap#3.1.1 (3.2.0 available)
│   └── jquery#2.1.1
→ portfolio ▌
```

Then, install the new version using the `bower install` command and followed by the Bower package name along with the version number. To install Bootstrap version 3.2.0, for example, run the `bower install bootstrap#3.2.0 --save` command.

 We actually should be able to update packages with the `bower update` command. Yet, it seems this command does not work as expected in accordance with a number of reports in the following Bower Issue thread (`https://github.com/bower/bower/issues/1054`). So, using the `bower install` command, as shown previously, is the way to go at the moment.

The portfolio website HTML structure

Now that we have put together the essential stuff to build the website. Let's start building the website's HTML structure. As in the last project, herein, we will be using a couple of new HTML5 elements to build the semantic structure.

Time for action – building the website HTML structure

In this section, we are going to build the website's HTML structure. You will find that a few of the elements that we are going to add herein will be similar to the ones we added in the first website, responsive blog. Hence, the following steps will be straightforward. If you have followed the first through to the end, these steps should also be easy to follow. Let's carry on.

1. Open `index.html`. Then, add the basic HTML structure, as follows:

```html
<!DOCTYPE html>
<html lang="en">
<head>
  <meta charset="UTF-8">
```

```
    <title>Portfolio</title>
  </head>
  <body>

  </body>
</html>
```

2. Below `<meta charset="UTF-8">`, add a meta tag to address the Internet Explorer rendering compatibility:

```
<meta http-equiv="X-UA-Compatible" content="IE=edge">
```

The preceding meta tag specification will force Internet Explorer to use the latest engine's version therein to render the page.

 For more in regard to `X-UA-Compatible`, refer to the Modern.IE article, *How to Use X-UA-Compatible* (`https://www.modern.ie/en-us/performance/how-to-use-x-ua-compatible`).

3. Below the `http-equiv` meta tag, add the meta viewport tag:

```
<meta name="viewport" content="width=device-width, initial-scale=1">
```

The preceding viewport meta tag specification defines the web page viewport width to follow the device viewport size, as well as scale the page at a ratio of 1:1 upon opening the web page the first time.

4. Below the viewport meta tag, add the link to the favicon and apple-touch-icon, which will display the website's icon in Apple devices, such as iPhone, iPad, and iPod:

```
<link rel="apple-touch-icon" href="assets/img/apple-icon.png">
<link rel="shortcut icon" href="assets/img/favicon.png" type="image/png">
```

5. Add the website's meta description below `<title>`:

```
<meta name="description" content="A simple portoflio website built using Bootstrap">
```

The description specified within this meta tag will be displayed in the **Search Engine Result Page (SERP)**.

6. You may also specify the author of the page with a meta tag below the meta description tag, as follows.

```
<meta name="author" content="Thoriq Firdaus">
```

7. Inside `<body>`, add the website off-canvas navigation HTML, as follows:

```
<nav id="menu" class="navmenu navmenu-inverse navmenu-fixed-left
offcanvas portfolio-menu" role="navigation">
        <ul class="nav navmenu-nav">
            <li class="active"><a href="#">Home</a></li>
            <li><a href="#">Blog</a></li>
            <li><a href="#">Shop</a></li>
            <li><a href="#">Speaking</a></li>
            <li><a href="#">Writing</a></li>
            <li><a href="#">About</a></li>
        </ul>
    </nav>
```

Aside from the essential classes that we have mentioned in the Jasny Bootstrap off-canvas section in this chapter, we have also added a new class named `portfolio-menu` in the `<nav>` element to apply our very own styles to the off-canvas navigation.

8. Add the Bootstrap `navbar` structure, along with `<button>` to slide the off-canvas in and out:

```
<div class="navbar navbar-default navbar-portfolio portfolio-
topbar">
<button type="button" class="navbar-toggle" data-
toggle="offcanvas" data-target="#menu" data-canvas="body">
        <span class="icon-bar"></span>
<span class="icon-bar"></span>
<span class="icon-bar"></span>
</button>
</div>
```

9. Below `navbar`, add the `<main>` element, as follows:

```
<main class="portfolio-main" id="content" role="main">
</main>
```

As described in W3C (`http://www.w3.org/TR/html-main-element/`), the `<main>` element defines the main content of the website. So, this is where we will put the website content including the portfolio images.

10. Add Bootstrap Jumbotron, containing the portfolio website name and a line of catchphrase. Since I will display the work of a friend of mine, Yoga Perdana, I wish to show off his name, along with his catchphrase that is displayed in his Dribbble page profile (`https://dribbble.com/yoga`), as follows:

```
<main class="portfolio-main" id="content" role="main">
<section class="jumbotron portfolio-about" id="about">
<h1 class="portfolio-name">Yoga Perdana</h1>
```

```
<p class="lead">Illustrator &amp; Logo designer. I work using
digital tools, specially vector.</p>
</section>
</main>
```

You may freely add your name or company name in this matter.

11. Below the Bootstrap Jumbotron section, add a new section with the HTML5 `<section>` element, along with a heading that defines this section, as follows:

```
. . .
<section class="jumbotron portfolio-about" id="about">
<h1 class="portfolio-name">Yoga Perdana</h1>
<p class="lead">Illustrator &amp; Logo designer. I work using
digital tools, specially vector.</p>
</section>
<section class="portfolio-display" id="portfolio">
  <h2>Portfolio</h2>
</section>
```

12. Add a Bootstrap container (`http://getbootstrap.com/css/#overview-container`) below the heading that will contain the portfolio images using the following code:

```
<section class="portfolio-display" id="portfolio">
<h2>Portfolio</h2>
    <div class="container">
</div>
</section>
```

13. Arrange the portfolio images into columns and rows. We have 12 portfolio images, which means we may have four images/columns in a row. The following is the first row:

```
. . .
<div class="container">
<div class="row">
<div class="col-md-3 col-sm-6 portfolio-item">
    <figure class="portfolio-image">
<img class="img-responsive" src="assets/img/6layers.jpg"
height="300" width="400" alt="">
<figcaption class="portfolio-caption">6 Layers</figcaption>
            </figure>
  </div>
<div class="col-md-3 col-sm-6 portfolio-item">
    <figure class="portfolio-image">
<img class="img-responsive" src="assets/img/blur.jpg" height="300"
width="400" alt="">
```

```
<figcaption class="portfolio-caption">Blur</figcaption>
</figure>
  </div>
<div class="col-md-3 col-sm-6 portfolio-item">
        <figure class="portfolio-image">
<img class="img-responsive" src="assets/img/brain.jpg"
height="300" width="400" alt="">
<figcaption class="portfolio-caption">Brain</figcaption>
</figure>
  </div>
  <div class="col-md-3 col-sm-6 portfolio-item">
      <figure class="portfolio-image">
<img class="img-responsive" src="assets/img/color.jpg"
height="300" width="400" alt="">
<figcaption class="portfolio-caption">Color</figcaption>
</figure>
  </div>
</div>
</div>
```

Each column is assigned with a special class to allow us to apply customized styles. We also added a class in `<figure>` that wraps the image, as well as the `<figcaption>` element that wraps the image caption for the same purpose.

14. Add the remaining images into columns and rows. Since, in this case, we have 12 images, there should be three rows displayed in the website. Each row contains four images, including one row that we've added in step 13.

15. Below the portfolio section, add the website message form containing three form fields and a button, as shown in the following code:

```
...
</section>
<div class="portfolio-contact" id="contact">
      <div class="container">
        <h2>Get in Touch</h2>
<form id="contact" method="post" class="form" role="form">
          <div class="form-group">
<input type="text" class="form-control input-lg" id="input-name"
placeholder="Name">
</div>
                <div class="form-group">
<input type="email" class="form-control input-lg" id="input-email"
placeholder="Email">
                </div>
                <div class="form-group">
```

```
<textarea class="form-control" rows="10"></textarea>
          </div>
  <button type="submit" class="btn btn-lg btn-primary">Submit</
button>
          </form>
</div>
</div>
```

Herein, we made the website form simple with only three form fields. But, you may add extra form fields, as per your own requirement.

16. Finally, we will add the website footer with the HTML5 `<footer>` element. The footer, as we have seen from the website wireframe, contains the social media icons and the website copyright statement.

17. Add the following HTML markup below the website's main content:

```
...
</main>
<footer class="portfolio-footer" id="footer">
        <div class="container">
          <div class="social" id="social">
            <ul>
<li class="twitter"><a class="icon ion-social-twitter"
href="#">Twitter</a></li>
<li class="dribbble"><a class="icon ion-social-dribbble-outline"
href="#">Dribbble</a></li>
                <ul>
          </div>
<div class="copyright">Yoga Perdana &copy; 2014</div>
        </div>
    </footer>
```

What just happened?

We just constructed the portfolio website HTML structure with a couple of HTML5 elements and Bootstrap reusable classes. You should be able to see the website through the following address http://localhost/portfolio/ or http://{computer-username}/ portfolio/ if you are using OS X. No styles have yet been applied to the website at this stage; we haven't linked any style sheet in the page. So, the screenshot following the upcoming tip is how the website looks currently.

The full code shown in the preceding steps can also be obtained from the following Gist `http://git.io/oIh31w`.

- Home
- Blog
- Shop
- Speaking
- Writing
- About

Yoga Perdana

Illustrator & Logo designer. I work using digital tools, specially vector.

Portfolio

6 Layers

Blur

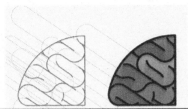

Have a go hero – extending the portfolio website

Bootstrap ships a variety of components. Yet, we use only a couple, including the grids, Jumbotron, buttons, and forms. Extend the website by adding extra Bootstrap components, as follows:

- Pagination (`http://getbootstrap.com/components/#pagination`)
- Breadcrumbs (`http://getbootstrap.com/components/#breadcrumbs`)
- Responsive embed (`http://getbootstrap.com/components/#responsive-embed`)
- Panels (`http://getbootstrap.com/components/#panels`)
- Wells (`http://getbootstrap.com/components/#wells`)

In addition, try creating more web pages and link them through the off-canvas navigation menus.

Pop quiz – Bootstrap button classes

Bootstrap specified a number of reusable classes to quickly shape and form elements with the preset styles.

Q1. Which of the following classes is not used in Bootstrap grid?

1. `col-sm-pull-8`
2. `col-md-push-3`
3. `col-xs-offset-5`
4. `col-lg-6`
5. `col-xl-7`

Q2. Which of the following classes does Bootstrap use to style a button?

1. `btn-link`
2. `btn-submit`
3. `btn-send`
4. `btn-cancel`
5. `btn-enter`

Summary

This chapter starts the second project of this book. We are building a portfolio website using one of the most popular frontend development frameworks, Bootstrap. We also explored a new enticing tool in web development named Bower, which streamlines the website dependencies management.

They both are a great combination of tools. Bootstrap lets us build responsive websites quickly with the modular components and reusable classes, while Bower makes the project more maintainable—easily.

In the next chapter, we will deal more with LESS and JavaScript to decorate the website.

6
Polishing the Responsive Portfolio Website with LESS

In the preceding chapter, we constructed the portfolio website structure with HTML5 and a couple of Bootstrap drop-in classes. The website as you might have seen isn't yet decorated. We haven't yet composed our very own styles or linked the style sheet to the page. So, this chapter's focus will be on website decoration.

Bootstrap primarily uses LESS to generate the styles of its components. Following suit, we will also use LESS to style the portfolio website. LESS brings a number of features, such as variables and mixins, that would allow us to write leaner and more efficient style rules. At the end of the day, you will also find customizing and maintaining website styles with LESS is easier than with plain CSS.

Furthermore, we've also used a Bootstrap extension called Jasny Bootstrap to include off-canvas navigation into the portfolio website. At this stage, nothing will happen to the off-canvas navigation; we only set out the HTML structure. So, in this chapter, apart from compiling the website styles, we will also compile the JavaScript library of both Bootstrap and Jasny Bootstrap to make the off-canvas navigation function.

In this chapter, we will discuss many things, including the following topics:

◆ Learn the basic LESS syntax, such as variables and mixins
◆ Organize the style sheet references with LESS `@import` directive
◆ Configure Koala to compile LESS into regular CSS

- ◆ Look into the source map to debug LESS
- ◆ Compose the website custom styles with LESS
- ◆ Compile JavaScript to activate off-canvas navigation

Basic LESS syntax

LESS (`http://lesscss.org/`) is a JavaScript-based CSS preprocessor developed by Alexis Sellier (`http://cloudhead.io/`), also known as CloudHead. As mentioned, Bootstrap uses LESS to compose its component styles¾though it only recently released the Sass version officially. As mentioned, we will follow Bootstrap to use LESS to compose our own style rules and manage style sheets.

In a nutshell, LESS extends CSS by bringing some programming features, such as variable, function, and operation. CSS is a straightforward language and fundamentally very easy to learn. However, maintaining static CSS is practically exhaustive, particularly when we have to deal with a thousand lines of style rules and multiple style sheets. The capabilities that LESS offers, such as variable, mixins, function, and operation (which we are going to take a look at shortly) will allow us to develop style rules that will be easier to maintain and organize.

Variables

A variable is the most fundamental feature in LESS. A variable in LESS, as in other programming languages, is used to store a constant or a value that can be reused later limitlessly within the entire style sheet. In LESS, a variable is declared with an @ sign and is followed by the variable name. The variable name can be a combination of numbers and letters. In the following example, we will create a couple of LESS variables to store some colors in the HEX format and assign them in the succeeding style rules to pass the colors, as shown in the following code:

```
@primaryColor: #234fb4;
@secondaryColor: #ffb400;
a {
  color: @primaryColor;
}
button {
  background-color: @secondaryColor;
}
```

Using a LESS compiler, such as Koala, the preceding codes will be compiled into static CSS, as follows:

```
a {
  color: #234fb4;
}
button {
  background-color: #ffb400;
}
```

Using variables is not only limited to storing colors as we just demonstrated. We can use variables for any type of values, for example:

```
@smallRadius: 3px;
```

One of the advantages of using a variable is that, if we have to make a change, we will only need to change the value within the variable. The change we make will take place in every occurrence of that variable in the style sheet. This is certainly a time saver. Scanning through the style sheet and making the change singly or perhaps with the **search** and **replace** feature of the code editor might cause unintended changes if not done carefully.

> You will find the term *compile* and *compiler* often. The word compile herein means that we convert the LESS into standard CSS format that can be rendered in the browser. Compiler is the tool used to do so. In this case, the tool we are using is Koala.

Nesting style rules

LESS lets us nest style rules into one another. Traditionally with plain CSS, when we want to apply style rules to elements, say, under a `<nav>` element, we can compose the style rules in the following way:

```
nav {
  background-color: #000;
  width: 100%;
}
nav ul {
  padding: 0;
  margin: 0;
}
nav li {
  display: inline;
}
```

As we can see from the preceding example, we repeat the `nav` selector each time we apply styles to a particular element nested under the `<nav>` element. By using LESS, we are able to eliminate this repetition and simplify it by nesting the style rules, as follows:

```less
nav {
   background-color: #000;
   width: 100%;
   ul {
      padding: 0;
      margin: 0;
   }
   li {
      display: inline;
   }
}
```

Eventually, the preceding style rules will return the same result—only we write the style rules more efficiently this time.

Mixins

Mixins are one of the most powerful features in LESS. Mixins simplify style rules declaration by allowing us to create a group of CSS properties that can be included in other style rules in the style sheets. Let's take a look at the following code snippet:

```less
.links {
   -webkit-border-radius: 3px;
   -mox-border-radius: 3px;
   border-radius: 3px;
   text-decoration: none;
   font-weight: bold;
}
.box {
-webkit-border-radius: 3px;
   -moz-border-radius: 3px;
   border-radius: 3px;
   position: absolute;
   top: 0;
   left: 0;
}
.button {
   -webkit-border-radius: 3px;
   -mox-border-radius: 3px;
   border-radius: 3px;
}
```

In the preceding example, we declared `border-radius` in three different style rules along with the vendor prefix to cover earlier versions of Firefox- and Webkit-based browsers. In LESS, we are able to simplify `border-radius` declaration by creating a mixin. A mixin in LESS is simply specified with a class selector. Given the preceding example, let's create a mixin named `.border-radius` to contain the `border-radius` properties, as follows:

```
.border-radius {
  -webkit-border-radius: 3px;
  -moz-border-radius: 3px;
  border-radius: 3px;
}
```

Afterwards, we include `.border-radius` into the succeeding style rules to pass the containing properties into them, as follows:

```
.links {
  .border-radius;
  text-decoration: none;
  font-weight: bold;
}
.box {
  .border-radius;
  position: absolute;
  top: 0;
  left: 0;
}
.button {
  .border-radius;
}
```

This code will produce exactly the same output as in the first code snippet of this section when compiled into static CSS.

Parametric mixins

Furthermore, we can also extend the mixins into so-called **parametric mixins**. This feature allows us to add arguments or variables and turn the mixins to be configurable. Let's take the same example as in the preceding section. But, this time, we will not assign a fixed value; instead, we replace it with a variable, as follows:

```
.border-radius (@radius) {
  -webkit-border-radius: @radius;
  -moz-border-radius: @radius;
  border-radius: @radius;
}
```

Now, we can insert this mixin into other style rules and assign a different value to each:

```
a {
  .border-radius(3px);
  text-decoration: none;
  font-weight: bold;
}
div {
  .border-radius(10px);
  position: absolute;
  top: 0;
  left: 0;
}
button {
  .border-radius(12px);
}
```

When we compile it into regular CSS, each style rule is applied with a different border-radius value, as follows:

```
a {
  -webkit-border-radius: 3px;
  -moz-border-radius: 3px;
  border-radius: 3px;
  text-decoration: none;
  font-weight: bold;
}
div {
  -webkit-border-radius: 10px;
  -moz-border-radius: 10px;
  border-radius: 10px;
  position: absolute;
  top: 0;
  left: 0;
}
button {
  -webkit-border-radius: 12px;
  -moz-border-radius: 12px;
  border-radius: 12px;
}
```

Specify a default value in a parametric mixin

Furthermore, we can specify a default value in a parametric mixin, which will be useful in case a parameter is not passed. When we set a parameter in a mixin, as we did in the preceding example, LESS will take the parameter as a requirement. If we do not pass a parameter in it, LESS will return an error. So, let's take the preceding example and extend it with a default value, say, 5px, as follows:

```
.border-radius(@radius: 5px) {
  -webkit-border-radius: @radius;
  -moz-border-radius: @radius;
  border-radius: @radius;
}
```

The preceding parametric mixin will return the border radius of 5px by default. The default value will be overwritten if we pass a custom value within brackets.

Merging mixins with extend syntax

Extend syntax is the long-awaited feature to come into LESS. One main issue with LESS mixins is that it simply copies the containing CSS properties of a mixin, thus producing duplicate code. Again, if we are dealing with a large-scale website with a thousand lines of codes, the amount of duplicated code would make the style sheet size unnecessarily large.

In Version 1.4, LESS introduced extend syntax. The extend syntax comes in a form that is similar to a CSS pseudo-class, :extend. The extend syntax will group CSS selectors that inherit the properties set containing the mixin. Compare the following two examples.

To begin with, we include a mixin without the :extend syntax:

```
.border-radius {
  -webkit-border-radius: 3px;
  -moz-border-radius: 3px;
  border-radius: 3px;
}
.box {
  .border-radius;
  position: absolute;
  top: 0;
  left: 0;
}
.button {
  .border-radius;
}
```

The preceding LESS code is short, but when it is compiled into CSS, the code extends to around 17 lines, as the `border-radius` properties are repeated or simply copied in every style rule, as follows:

```
.border-radius {
  -webkit-border-radius: 3px;
  -moz-border-radius: 3px;
  border-radius: 3px;
}
.box {
  -webkit-border-radius: 3px;
  -moz-border-radius: 3px;
  border-radius: 3px;
  position: absolute;
  top: 0;
  left: 0;
}
.button {
  -webkit-border-radius: 3px;
  -moz-border-radius: 3px;
  border-radius: 3px;
}
```

In this second example, we will put the `:extend` syntax into practice into the same mixin:

```
.border-radius {
  -webkit-border-radius: 3px;
  -moz-border-radius: 3px;
  border-radius: 3px;
}
.box {
  &:extend(.border-radius);
  position: absolute;
  top: 0;
  left: 0;
}
.button {
  &:extend(.border-radius);
}
```

The following is how the code turns into plain CSS; it becomes even shorter than the initial uncompiled LESS codes.

```
.border-radius,
.box
```

```
.button {
  -webkit-border-radius: 3px;
  -moz-border-radius: 3px;
  border-radius: 3px;
}
.box {
  position: absolute;
  top: 0;
  left: 0;
}
```

Generating value with mathematical operations

We can also perform math operations with LESS-like addition, subtraction, division, and multiplication. Operations could be pretty useful to determine a length, such as the element's width and height. In the following example, we will calculate the proper box width by subtracting it with the padding so that it can be fit into the parent container.

First, we will define the variable for the padding with the `@padding` variable:

```
@padding: 10px;
```

Then, we specify the box width and subtract it with the `@padding` variable:

```
.box {
  padding: @padding;
  width: 500px - (@padding * 2);
}
```

Remember that the padding takes two sides of the box, whether it is right and left or top and bottom, so that is why we multiply `@padding` in the width property by two. Finally when we compile this LESS operation into the regular CSS, this code will look as follows:

```
.box {
  padding: 10px;
  width: 480px;
}
```

In other cases, we can do the same to the height property, as follows:

```
.box {
  padding: @padding;
  width: 500px - (@padding * 2);
  height: 500px - (@padding * 2);
}
```

Generating color with mathematical operations and LESS functions

Believe it or not, in LESS, we can alter colors with math operations. It's like mixing paint colors, except we do it by addition, subtraction, division, and multiplication. For instance:

```
.selector {
  color: #aaa + 2;
}
```

When compiled, the color turns into the following:

```
.selector {
  color: #acacac;
}
```

Furthermore, LESS also provides a handful of functions that allow us to turn colors darker or lighter to a certain extent. The following example will lighten the color in the @color variable by 50%.

```
@color: #FF0000;
.selector {
  color: lighten(@color, 50%);
}
```

Alternatively, to darken the color, use the darken() function, as follows:

```
@color: #FF0000;
.selector {
  color: darken(@color, 50%);
}
```

 A complete list of the LESS color function can be found in the following page of LESS's official website (http://lesscss.org/functions/#color-operations).

Referential import

This is one of my favorite features in LESS. The referential import, as the name implies, allows us to import an external style sheet merely as reference. Prior to the emerging of this feature, all style rules in the style sheet imported with the @import directive will be appended, which is more often than not unnecessary.

Since Version 1.5, LESS introduced the (reference) option that marks @import as reference, thus preventing the external style rules from being appended. Add the (reference) mark after @import, as follows:

```
@import (reference) 'partial.less';
```

Using a variable in an import statement

One of the constraints that LESS used to encounter was when using a variable within the @import directive (https://github.com/less/less.js/issues/410). It is one of the most requested features to present in LESS and finally has been resolved since LESS 1.4. We are now able to declare a variable in an @import statement by naming the variable within curly braces, for example, @{variable-name}.

The use of a variable along with @import will allow us to define the style sheet path once, through a variable. Then, call the path using the variable, as follows:

```
@path: 'path/folder/less/';
@import '@{path}mixins.less';
@import '@{path}normalize.less';
@import '@{path}print.less';
```

This approach is visibly neater and more efficient than having to add the full path every time we import a new style sheet, as follows:

```
@import 'path/folder/less/mixins.less';
@import 'path/folder/less/normalize.less';
@import 'path/folder/less/print.less';
```

> Refer to the **Import Directive** section of the LESS official website (http://lesscss.org/features/#import-directives-feature) for further assistance on importing an external style sheet with LESS.

Using source map for easier style debugging

While CSS preprocessors like LESS allows us to write style rules more efficiently, the browsers are still only able to read plain CSS, which will cause a new problem particularly when debugging issues in the style sheet.

Since the browser is referring to the generated CSS instead of the source file (LESS), we will likely be clueless of the exact lines where the style rules are actually declared in a source file. A source map addresses this issue by mapping the generated CSS back to the source files. In a browser that supports source map, you will find the browser refers directly to the source file. In the case of LESS, the browser will refer to the `.less` style sheet as shown in the following screenshot:

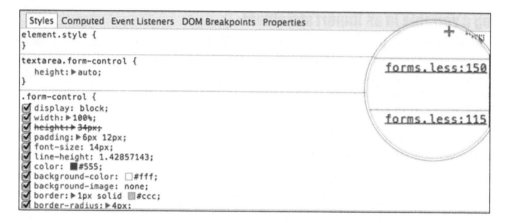

In this project, we will generate a source map of the generated CSS. So, if we encounter bugs, it is a lot easier to address it. We can immediately figure out exactly where the style rules reside.

Head over to the following references for further information about the source map:

- Working with CSS preprocessors by Google (https://developer.chrome.com/devtools/docs/css-preprocessors)
- An Introduction to Source Map (http://blog.teamtreehouse.com/introduction-source-maps)
- Using LESS Source Maps (http://roots.io/using-less-source-maps/)

More on LESS

LESS has plenty of features and will only grow with more additions in the years to come. It's impractical to include and discuss them all at once in this book. So, the following are a few references to dig in deeper:

- ♦ LESS's official website (`http://lesscss.org/`); the best source to be up-to-date with LESS

- ♦ *LESS Web Development Essentials, Bass Jobsen, Packt Publishing* (`https://www.packtpub.com/web-development/less-web-development-essentials`)

- ♦ Instant LESS CSS preprocessor (`https://www.packtpub.com/web-development/instant-less-css-preprocessor-how-instant`)

External style sheet references

We walked through a big amount of basic syntax in LESS in the preceding section. Now, we will start to actually work with LESS, speaking of which, before we are able to write our own style rules as well as reuse variables, mixins, and functions that are shipped in Bootstrap and the Jasny Bootstrap package, we will have to import them into our own style sheet with the LESS `@import` directive.

Time for action – creating style sheets and organizing external style sheet references

Perform the following steps to manage the style sheet references:

1. Go to the project directory and create a new style sheet named `var-bootstrap.less` in `assets/less` directory. This style sheet contains the copy of Bootstrap's predefined variables. This copy will allow us to customize the variables without affecting the initial specifications.

2. Hence, copy the Bootstrap variables in the `variables.less` style sheet of the `/bootstrap/less` directory. Paste the complete variables into `var-bootstrap.less` that we only created in step 1.

 For your convenience, you may also copy Bootstrap variables directly from the Github repository (`http://git.io/7LmzGA`).

3. Create a new style sheet named `var-jasny.less`. Similar to `var-bootstrap.less`, this style sheet will contain the copy of the Jasny Bootstrap variables.

4. Obtain the Jasny Bootstrap variables in `variables.less` of the `jasny-bootstrap/less` directory. Paste all the variables in the `var-jasny.less` style sheet we just created in step 3.

> Alternatively, copy the variables directly from the Jasny Bootstrap repository (`http://git.io/SK1ccg`).

5. Create a new style sheet named `frameworks.less`.

6. We are going to use this style sheet to import the Bootstrap and Jasny Bootstrap style sheets residing in the `bower_component` folder.

7. In `frameworks.less`, create a variable named `@path-bootstrap` to define the path, pointing to the folder named `less`, where all the LESS style sheets of Bootstrap reside:

```
@path-bootstrap: '../../bower_components/bootstrap/less/';
```

8. Similarly, create a variable that defines the path, pointing to the Jasny Bootstrap `less` folder, as follows:

```
@path-jasny: '../../bower_components/jasny-bootstrap/less/';
```

9. Also create one to define the Ionicons path:

```
@path-ionicons: '../../bower_components/ionicons-less/less/';
```

10. Import the style sheets that contain variables using the following code:

```
@import 'var-bootstrap.less';
@import 'var-jasny.less';
```

11. Import the Bootstrap and Jasny Bootstrap style sheets, which are only required to build the portfolio website. Specify the paths using the variables we created in steps 6 to 8, as follows:

```
// Mixins
@import '@{path-bootstrap}mixins.less';

// Reset
@import '@{path-bootstrap}normalize.less';
@import '@{path-bootstrap}print.less';

// Core CSS
@import '@{path-bootstrap}scaffolding.less';
@import '@{path-bootstrap}type.less';
@import '@{path-bootstrap}grid.less';
@import '@{path-bootstrap}forms.less';
@import '@{path-bootstrap}buttons.less';

// Icons
```

```less
@import '@{path-ionicons}ionicons.less';

// Components
@import '@{path-bootstrap}navs.less';
@import '@{path-bootstrap}navbar.less';
@import '@{path-bootstrap}jumbotron.less';

// Offcanvas
@import "@{path-jasny}navmenu.less";
@import "@{path-jasny}offcanvas.less";

// Utility classes
@import '@{path-bootstrap}utilities.less';
@import '@{path-bootstrap}responsive-utilities.less';
```

 You can also copy the preceding code from Gist (`http://git.io/WpBVAA`).

 To minimize extraneous style rules, which really are not needed for the website, we excluded a number of Bootstrap and Jasny Bootstrap style sheets from `frameworks.less` as you can see previously.

12. Create a new style sheet named `style.less`. This is the style sheet where we are going to compose our very own style rules.

13. Import the Bootstrap variables and the mixins within `style.less`:

```less
@path-bootstrap: '../../bower_components/bootstrap/less/';
@import 'var-bootstrap.less';
@import 'var-jasny.less';
@import (reference) '@{path-bootstrap}mixins.less';
```

What just happened?

To sum up, we just created style sheets and put them in order. At first, we created two style sheets named `var-bootstrap.less` and `var-jasny.less` to store the Bootstrap and Jasny Bootstrap variables. As mentioned, we made these copies to avoid directly altering the originals. We have also created a style sheet named `frameworks.less`, containing references to the Bootstrap and Jasny Bootstrap style sheets.

Finally, we created the website primary style sheet named `style.less` and imported the variables and mixins so that they are reusable inside the `style.less`.

Have a go hero – name and organize the style sheets

In the preceding steps, we organized and named the folders as well as the files to my personal preferences. Even so, you don't have to follow the naming conventions absolutely. Do organize and name them in your own way.

 The most important thing to note is that the @import statement refers to the correct file name.

The following are a few ideas:

◆ Rename `var-bootstrap.less` to simply `vars.less`.

◆ Alternatively, create a new folder name `vars` or `configs` to put the `var-bootstrap.less` and `var-jasny.less` style sheet in it.

◆ Did you know that you can also import the LESS style sheet without declaring the `.less` extension. For the sake of simplicity, you can omit the extensions, for example:

```
@import (reference) '@{path-bootstrap}mixins.less';
```

Pop quiz – which of the following option is not LESS Import option?

Q1. In one of the section of this chapter, we discussed `(reference)`, which imports yet treats external LESS style sheets only as a reference. In addition to `(reference)`, LESS also provides more options to import a style sheet. So, which of the following is not the LESS import option?

1. `(less)`
2. `(css)`
3. `(multiple)`
4. `(once)`
5. `(default)`

Q2. How do you use variable within an `@import` statement?

1. `@import '@{variable}style.less';`
2. `@import '@[variable]style.less';`
3. `@import '@(variable)style.less';`

Working with Koala

The HTML and the style sheets have been prepared. It's now time to put them together to shape a solid portfolio website. We will compose the website styles using LESS syntax. Herein, we will also use Koala as in the first project. This time, we will compile LESS into plain CSS.

Time for action – compiling LESS into CSS using Koala

Perform the following steps to compile LESS into CSS using Koala:

1. Add the project directory in the Koala sidebar, as follows:

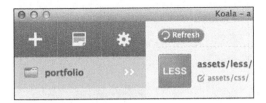

2. Select all the style sheets except `frameworks.less` and `style.less`. Right-click and select **Toggle Auto Compile**. Have a look at the following screenshot:

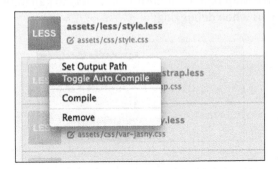

This will turn off the **Auto Compile** option on the selected style sheets and prevent Koala from compiling these style sheet unintentionally.

3. On the other hand, ensure that **Auto Compile** is checked for the two remaining style sheets, `frameworks.less` and `style.less`:

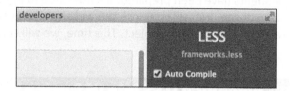

4. Make sure that the `frameworks.less` and `style.less` output is set to `/assets/css` directory, as shown in the following screenshot:

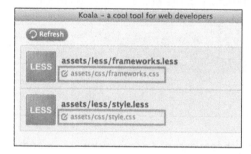

5. Check the **Source Map** option for both style sheets to generate the source map files, which will help us when debugging:

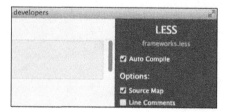

6. Select the output styles for the two style sheets, `frameworks.less` and `style.less`, to **compress**:

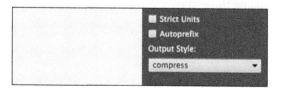

This option will generate a small-sized CSS style sheet, as the codes within the style sheet will be compressed into a single line. Hence, the style sheet will load faster in the browser and also save bandwidth consumption on the user's side.

7. Select `frameworks.less` and click on the **Compile** button to compile it into CSS:

8. Do the same for `style.less`. Select it and click on the **Compile** button to compile it into CSS. Open `index.html` in the code editor, and link both of the style sheets inside `<head>`, as follows:

    ```
    <link href="assets/css/frameworks.css" rel="stylesheet">
    <link href="assets/css/style.css" rel="stylesheet">
    ```

What just happened?

In the preceding steps, we compiled the website primary style sheets, `frameworks.less` and `style.less`, from LESS to CSS. You should now have them along with the source maps in the `assets/css/` directory. The code is compressed, thus resulting in a relatively small file size, as shown in the following screenshot:

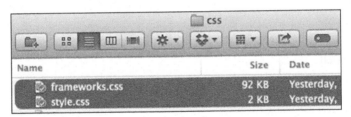

The style sheets are relatively small in size. As shown, frameworks.css is 92 kb, while style.css is only 2 kb

Additionally, we also linked these CSS style sheets in `index.html`. However, since we have not yet written our own styles, the websites are decorated with the default Bootstrap styles, as shown in the following screenshot:

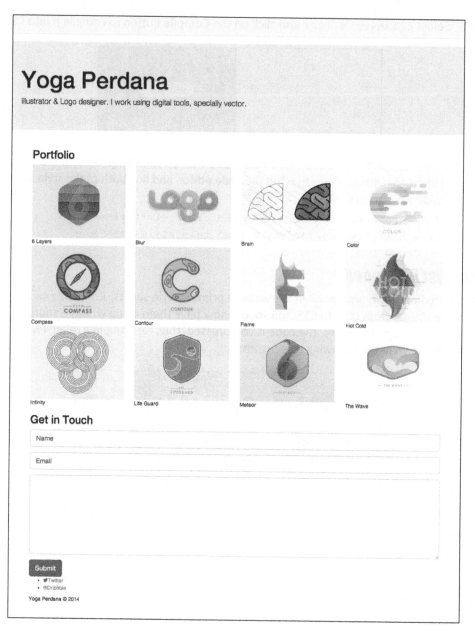

Polishing the portfolio website with LESS

This is the section you might be waiting for, to style the portfolio website. It is apparently a pleasing experience to see the website start to have shapes, colors, and look. In this section, we will customize the default styles and compose our style rules using the LESS syntax that we have covered earlier in this chapter.

Time for action – composing the website styles with LESS syntax

Perform the following steps to style the website:

1. Add a new font family from Google Font. Herein, I opted for Varela Round (`http://www.google.com/fonts/specimen/Varela+Round`). Place the following Google Font link before any other style sheets:

   ```
   <link href='http://fonts.googleapis.com/css?family=Varela+Round'
   rel='stylesheet' type='text/css'>
   ```

2. We will customize the default styles by changing some variables. Open `var-bootstrap.less` in Sublime Text. First, we change the `@brand-primary` variable that defines the Bootstrap primary color; change it from `#428bca` to `#46acb8`:

3. Also, change the color in the `@brand-success` variable from `#5cb85c` to `#7ba47c`:

4. Change the `@headings-font-family` variable, which defines the font family used in the headings, from `inherit` to `"Varela Round"`, as follows:

   ```
   @headings-font-family: "Varela Round", @font-family-sans-serif;
   ```

5. The Bootstrap default style shows a glowing effect when the user focusses on a form field. The color of this effect is specified in `@input-border-focus`. Change the color from `#66afe9` to `#89c6cb`:

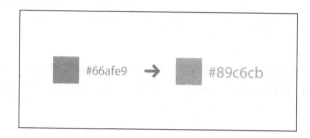

6. In the top section of the website, you can see that the navbar still has the Bootstrap default style with the gray background and border color, as shown in the following screenshot:

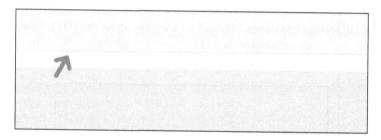

7. These two colors are specified in `@navbar-default-bg` and `@navbar-default-border`, respectively. Change both of these variable values to transparent, as follows:

```
@navbar-default-bg: transparent;
@navbar-default-border: transparent;
```

8. Similarly, the default style of the Jumbotron section is set with a gray background color. To remove this color, set the `@jumbotron-bg` variable to `transparent`, as follows:

```
@jumbotron-bg: transparent;
```

9. We will be back editing a few more Bootstrap variables later on. For the meantime, let's write our own style rules. To begin with, we will show the navbar toggle button, which is hidden by the Bootstrap default styles. In our case, this button will be used to slide the off-canvas navigation on and off. Let's force this button to be visible with the following style rules:

```
.portfolio-topbar {
  .navbar-toggle {
```

```
    display: block;
  }
}
```

10. As you can see from the following screenshot, the toggle button with the so-called hamburger icon (`http://gizmodo.com/who-designed-the-iconic-hamburger-icon-1555438787`) is now visible:

11. Currently, this button is positioned on the right-hand side. Referring to the website blueprint, it should be on the left. Add `float:left` to put it on the left-hand side and `margin-left:15px` to add a little whitespace to the button's left, as follows:

```
.portfolio-topbar {
  .navbar-toggle {
    display: block;
    float: left;
    margin-left: 15px;
  }
}
```

12. Herein, I want to customize the toggle button's default styles, which are also specified through a couple of variables in `var-bootstrap.less`. Hence, open `var-bootstrap.less` in Sublime Text.

13. First of all, we will remove the button borders by changing the value of the `@navbar-default-toggle-border-color` variable from #ddd to `transparent`, as follows:

```
@navbar-default-toggle-border-color: transparent;
```

14. We will also remove the gray background color that appears when we hover over the button. Remove the gray background color out of it by changing the `@navbar-default-toggle-hover-bg` variable from #ddd to `transparent`, as follows:

```
@navbar-default-toggle-hover-bg: transparent;
```

15. I want the hamburger icon to look bolder and strong. So, herein, we want to change the colors to black. Change the value of `@navbar-default-toggle-icon-bar-bg` from `#888` to `#000`:

```
@navbar-default-toggle-icon-bar-bg: #000;
```

16. At this stage, the website content is aligned to the left-hand side, which is the default browser alignment for any content. Following the website blueprint, the website content should be centered. Use `text-align: center`, as follows, to align the content to the center:

```
.portfolio-about,
.portfolio-display,
.portfolio-contact,
.portfolio-footer {
  text-align: center;
}
```

17. Add the following to turn the website name to all-caps (all capital letters), making it bigger and bolder:

```
.portfolio-about {
  .portfolio-name {
    text-transform: uppercase;
  }
}
```

18. On the other hand, make the catchphrase line subtler by specifying the text color to gray light. Herein, we can simply use Bootstrap's predefined variable named `@gray-light` to apply the gray color, as follows:

```
.portfolio-about {
  .portfolio-name {
    text-transform: uppercase;
  }
  .lead {
    color: @gray-light;
  }
}
```

19. In the portfolio section, specify the background color with gray light, which is lighter than the color in `@gray-lighter` variable. The addition of the background color aims to lay a bit of emphasis on the portfolio section.

20. In this project, we opt to use the LESS `darken()` function to slightly darken the white color, as follows:

```
.portfolio-display {
  background-color: darken(#fff, 1%);
}
```

The background color may alternatively be achieved by lightening the black color by 99 percent using the LESS `lighten()` function as `background-color: lighten(#000, 99%);`.

21. At this stage, if we take a look at the portfolio section, it seems there are merely little spaces at the top and the bottom, as pointed out in the following screenshot:

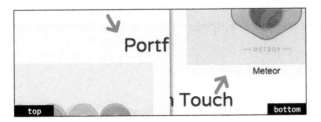

22. Give the portfolio section more space to breathe at the top and bottom by adding `padding-top` and `padding-bottom`, as follows:

```
.portfolio-display {
  background-color: darken(#fff, 1%);
padding-top: 60px;
  padding-bottom: 60px;
}
```

23. To sum up, we added two headings in the website, including one in the portfolio section, to explicitly display the section name. These headings will share the same style rules. So, in that case, we better create a mixin that specifically defines the heading styles.

24. Define the mixin as well as the CSS properties to apply the heading styles, as follows:

```
.heading {
  color: lighten(#000, 70%);
  text-transform: uppercase;
  font-size: 21px;
  margin-bottom: 60px;
}
```

25. Add the following style rules for the section heading, which will make it look subtler and in tune with the background color of the portfolio section:

```
.portfolio-display {
...
  h2 {
    &:extend(.heading);
  }
}
```

26. As shown in the following screenshot, there is only very little space in between each row; the rows are too close to each other, as follows:

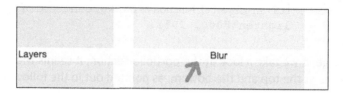

So, put more space by specifying `margin-bottom` for each portfolio item, as follows:

```
.portfolio-item {
  margin-bottom: 30px;
}
```

27. Add styles for the portfolio image, as follows:

```
.portfolio-image {
  padding: 15px;
  background-color: #fff;
margin-right: auto;
margin-left: auto;
}
```

28. Also, add the styles for the caption, as follows:

```
.portfolio-caption {
  font-weight: 500;
  margin-top: 15px;
  color: @gray;
}
```

29. What do you think about showing a transition effect when we hover over the portfolio image? That will look nice, won't it? In this case, I would like to show a shadow surrounding the portfolio image upon hover.

30. Add the effect using Bootstrap's predefined mixins, `.transition()` and `.box-shadow()`, as follows:

```
.portfolio-image {
  padding: 15px;
  background-color: #fff;
margin-right: auto;
margin-left: auto;
  .transition(box-shadow 1s);
  &:hover {
    .box-shadow(0 0 8px fade(#000, 10%));
  }
}
```

31. Below the portfolio section, we have the website contact form, which has already been applied with the Bootstrap default styling. So, let's customize it with our own style rules.

32. First, we will add more spaces at the top and the bottom of the contact form section with `padding`.

33. Add the styles for the heading with the `.heading` mixin we created in step 18:

```
.portfolio-contact {
  . . .
  h2 {
    &:extend(.heading);
  }
}
```

34. The form currently spans the container fully. So, add the following style rules to set the maximum width, yet still display the form in the middle of the container, as follows:

```
.portfolio-contact {
  . . .
  .form {
    width: 100%;
    max-width: 600px;
    margin-right: auto;
    margin-left: auto;
  }
}
```

35. Add the following style rules to make the form elements—`<input>`, `<textarea>`, `<button>`—look flatter. These style rules remove the shadow and lower the border radius. Have a look at the following code:

```
.portfolio-contact {
  . . .
  .form {
    width: 100%;
    max-width: 600px;
    margin-right: auto;
    margin-left: auto;
    input, textarea, button {
      box-shadow: none;
      border-radius: @border-radius-small;
    }
  }
}
```

36. Add the following lines to style the button and make it live with a transition effect, as follows:

```
.portfolio-contact {
...
  .form {
    width: 100%;
    max-width: 600px;
    margin-right: auto;
    margin-left: auto;
    input, textarea, button {
      box-shadow: none;
      border-radius: @border-radius-small;
    }
    .btn {
      display: block;
      width: 100%;
      .transition(background-color 500ms);
    }
  }
}
```

37. Starting this step, we will add style rules for the footer, the last section of the website. The footer contains the social media links, Dribbble and Twitter, and a copyright statement at the very bottom.

38. First, as in the preceding sections, we put more whitespace at the top and bottom of the section with padding:

```
.portfolio-footer {
  padding-top: 60px;
  padding-bottom: 60px;
}
```

39. Then, we put more spaces between the social media links and the copyright statement with `margin-bottom`:

```
.portfolio-footer {
  padding-top: 60px;
  padding-bottom: 60px;
  .social {
    margin-bottom: 30px;
  }
}
```

40. Add the following lines to remove the `<ul>` element `padding` derived from default browser styles:

```
.portfolio-footer {
  ...
  .social {
    margin-bottom: 30px;
    ul {
      padding-left: 0;
    }
  }
}
```

41. Add the highlighted lines in the following code to display the social media links beside each other:

```
.portfolio-footer {
  ...
  .social {
    margin-bottom: 30px;
    ul {
      padding-left: 0;
    }
    li {
      list-style: none;
      display: inline-block;
      margin: 0 15px;
    }
  }
}
```

42. Give the social media links the color of their respective social media brands, as follows:

```
.portfolio-footer {
  ...
  .social {
    ...
    a {
      font-weight: 600;
      color: @gray;
      text-decoration: none;
      .transition(color 500ms);
      &:before {
        display: block;
        font-size: 32px;
        margin-bottom: 5px;
      }
    }
```

```
.twitter a:hover {
  color: #55acee;
}
.dribbble a:hover {
  color: #ea4c89;
}
}
}
```

[
Get more colors of popular websites in BrandColors
(http://brandcolors.net/).
]

43. Finally, make the copyright statement color subtler with the gray color:

```
.portfolio-footer {
...
  .copyright {
    color: @gray-light;
  }
}
```

What just happened?

In the preceding steps, we just styled the website by customizing a number of Bootstrap variables as well as composing our own style rules. Compile style.less to generate the CSS. Additionally, you can obtain all the style rules we applied from this Gist (http://git.io/-FWuiQ).

The website should now be presentable. The following screenshot shows how the website looks in the desktop view:

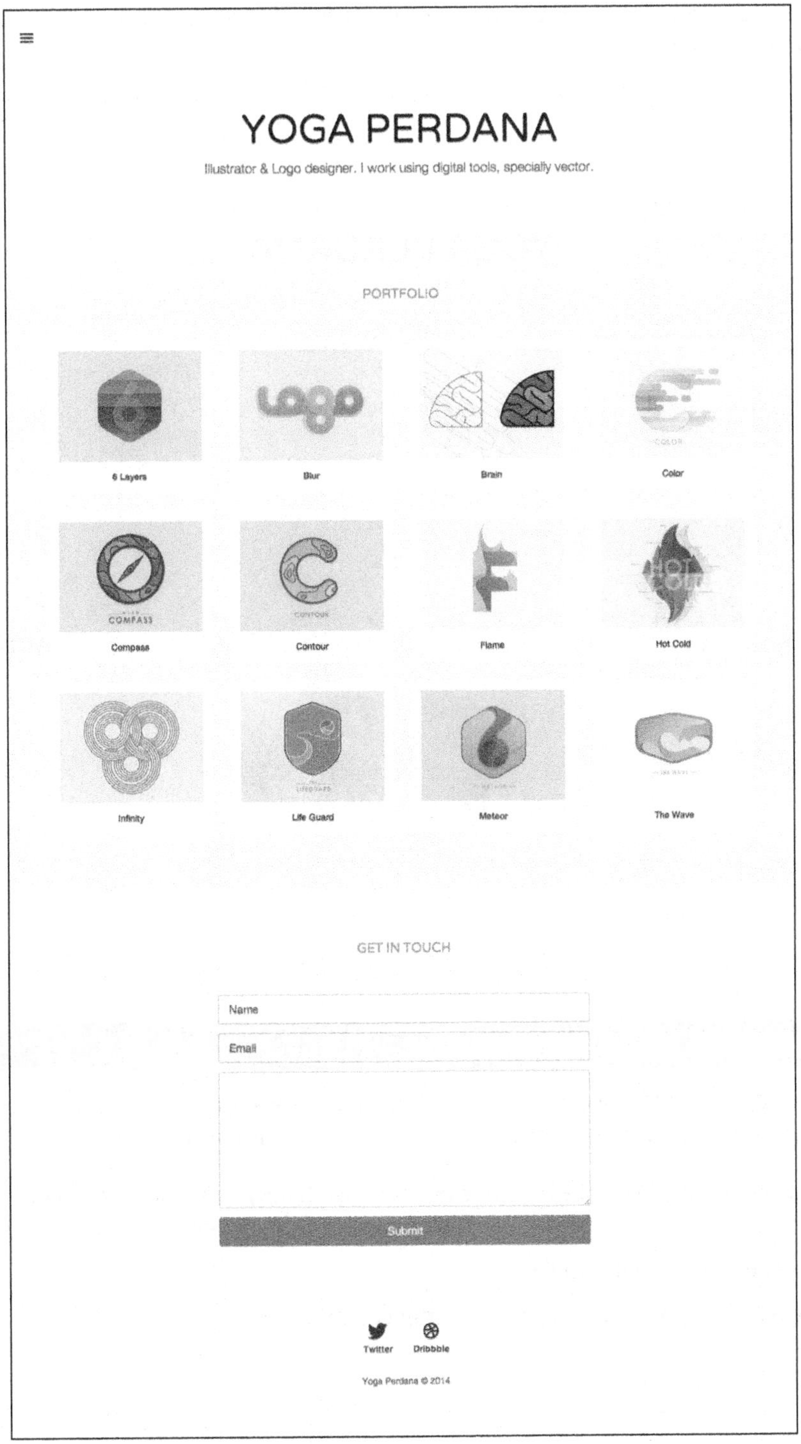

YOGA PERDANA

Illustrator & Logo designer. I work using digital tools, specially vector.

PORTFOLIO

6 Layers

Blur

Brain

Color

Compass

Contour

Flame

Hot Cold

Infinity

Life Guard

Meteor

The Wave

GET IN TOUCH

Name

Email

Submit

Twitter   Dribbble

The website is also responsive; the layout will adapt to the viewport width size, as shown in the following screenshot:

Have a go hero – being more creative

Many of the style rules that we have just applied in the preceding section are merely decorative. Feel free to add more creativity and customization, as follows:

- ◆ Explore the website's new color schemes. Use handy tools, such as Kuler, (`https://kuler.adobe.com/`) to generate color scheme
- ◆ Apply different font families
- ◆ Present more awesome transition effects with CSS3

Pop quiz — using LESS function and extend syntax

Q1. How do you make a color lighter with LESS?

1. `lighter(#000, 30%);`

2. `lighten(#000, 30%);`

3. `lightening(#000, 30%);`

Q2. How do you make a color transparent?

1. `fadeout(#000, 10%);`

2. `transparentize(#000, 10%);`

3. `fade-out(#000, 10%);`

Q3. Which one of the following is an incorrect way to extend a mixin in LESS?

1. `.class:extend(.another-class);`

2. `.class::extend(.another-class);`

3. ```
   .class {
   :extend(.another-class);
   }
   ```

Improve and make the website functioning with JavaScript

The off-canvas navigation has not yet been activated. If you click on the toggle button, the off-canvas navigation will not slide in. Furthermore, if you view the portfolio website in Internet Explorer 8, you will find that a number of style rules are not applied. This is because Internet Explorer 8 does not recognize the HTML5 elements that are used in the website. To sort these issues out, we will have to make use of some JavaScript libraries..

Time for action – compiling JavaScript with Koala

1. Create a new JavaScript file named `html5shiv.js` in `assets/js` directory.

2. Import `html5shiv.js` from the HTML5Shiv package we downloaded through Bower into this file:

   ```
   // @koala-prepend "../../bower_components/html5shiv/dist/
   html5shiv.js"
   ```

3. Create a new JavaScript file named `bootstrap.js`.
   ```

4. In `bootstrap.js`, import the JavaScript libraries that are required to turn the off-canvas navigation functionality on, as follows:

```
// @koala-prepend "../../bower_components/jquery/dist/jquery.js"
// @koala-prepend "../../bower_components/bootstrap/js/transition.
js"
// @koala-prepend "../../bower_components/jasny-bootstrap/js/
offcanvas.js"
```

5. Open Koala and ensure that the **Auto Compile** option for `html5shiv.js` and `bootstrap.js` is checked, as shown in the following screenshot:

6. Also, make sure that the output path of these two JavaScript files is set to the `/assets/js` directory, as shown in the following screenshot:

7. Compile both these JavaScript files by clicking on the **Compile** button in Koala, as follows:

Once these JavaScript files are compiled, you should find the minified version of these files, `html5shiv.min.js` and `bootstrap.min.js`, as shown in the following screenshot:

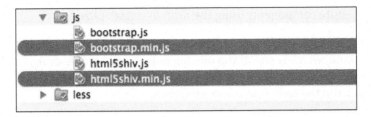

8. Open `index.html` in Sublime Text, and link `html5shiv.js` within the `<head>` section using the Internet Explorer conditional comment tag, as follows:

```
<!--[if lt IE 9]>
<script type="text/javascript" src="assets/js/html5shiv.min.js"></
script>
<![endif]-->
```

9. Link `bootstrap.min.js` at the bottom of `index.html`, as follows:

```
<script type="text/javascript" src="assets/js/bootstrap.min.js"></
script>
```

What just happened?

We just compiled jQuery and Bootstrap JavaScript libraries to enable the off-canvas functionality. We also enabled HTML5 elements in Internet Explorer 8 using HTML5Shiv. By now, the website is fully functional.

 You can view the website through this Github page (`http://tfirdaus.github.io/rwd-portfolio/`).

You should be able to slide in and out the off-canvas navigation, and the styles should now be visible in Internet Explorer 8. Take a look at the following screenshot:

The off-canvas navigation menu is slid in.

Summary

We just accomplished the second project of this book. In this project, we built a portfolio website using Bootstrap. Bootstrap makes it easy and quick to build a responsive website along with the website components using the drop-in classes provided.

At the top of that, we also used a Bootstrap extension called Jasny Bootstrap to include off-canvas navigation, which is one of the missing popular responsive design patterns in the original Bootstrap. When it comes styling the website, we used LESS, a CSS preprocessor that allows us to write the style rules more efficiently.

To sum up, we did many things in this project to get the website up and running. I hope you've learned many things along the way.

In the next chapter, we will start off the third project of this book using the Foundation framework. Stay tuned!

7
A Responsive Website for Business with Foundation

In this era, where many people are connected to the Internet, having a website becomes an essential for a company of any size—a small company or a Fortune 500 company with multibillion businesses. Therefore, in this third project of this book, we are going to build a responsive website for business.

To build the website, we will adopt a new framework called Foundation. Foundation is built by ZURB, a web-development agency based in California. It's a meticulously crafted framework with a stack of interactive widgets. On the technical side, Foundation styles are built on top of Sass and SCSS. Hence, we will also walk through the subject during the course of working on the project.

To work towards this project, first let's assume that you have a business idea. It might be a bit exaggerated, but it's a brilliant idea that could potentially turn into a multibillion-dollar business and change the world. You have an awesome product baked, and now it's time to build the website. You are very excited and cannot wait to rock the world.

So, without further ado, let's get the project started.

This chapter will primarily revolve around Foundation, and the topics that we are going to cover herein include:

- Examining the website design and layout in wireframe
- Looking into Foundation features, components, and add-ons
- Managing the project directories and assets
- Obtaining the Foundation package through Bower
- Constructing the website HTML structure

Examining the website layout

First and foremost, unlike the previous two projects we did, we are going to examine the website layout in wireframe before going any further in the chapter. After examining it, we will discover the Foundation components that are required for the website, along with the components and assets that may not be available in the Foundation package. The following is the website layout in the normal desktop screen size:

| Logo | | features | pricing | blog | login | sign up |

Lorem ipsum dolor sit.

Lorem ipsum dolor sit amet, consectetur adipisicing elit,
sed do eiusmod tempor incididunt ut labore et dolore
magna aliqua.

| Button |

Lorem ipsum dolor sit amet,
consectetur adipisicing elit, sed do
eiusmod tempor incididunt ut labore
et dolore magna aliqua.

Lorem ipsum dolor sit amet,
consectetur adipisicing elit, sed do
eiusmod tempor incididunt ut labore
et dolore magna aliqua.

Lorem ipsum dolor sit amet,
consectetur adipisicing elit, sed do
eiusmod tempor incididunt ut labore
et dolore magna aliqua.

Lorem ipsum dolor sit amet,
consectetur adipisicing elit, sed do
eiusmod tempor incididunt ut labore
et dolore magna aliqua.

Lorem ipsum dolor sit amet, consectetur adipisicing elit, sed do
eiusmod tempor incididunt ut labore et dolore magna aliqua.

Basic	Team	Enterprise
$10/month	**$50/month**	**$300/month**
• 1Gb Storage • 1 User • 24/7 Support	• 50 Gb Storage • Up to 10 Users • 24/7 Support	• Unlimited Storage • Unlimited Users • 25/7 Priority Support
Sign Up	Sign Up	Sign Up

| about | contact | help | careers | terms | privacy |

Facebook   Twitter

Copyright 2014 Super Awesome App. All rights reserved.

The preceding wireframe shows that the website will have five sections. The first section, plainly, is the header. The header section will contain the website logo, menu navigation, a few lines of catchphrases, and a button—many call it a call-to-action button.

 The following are a couple of references in regard to guidelines, best practices, and examples of call-to-action buttons. These are old posts, yet the underlying guidelines, tips, and principles are timeless; it's still valid and relevant to date.

- Call to Action Buttons: Examples and Best Practices (`http://www.smashingmagazine.com/2009/10/13/call-to-action-buttons-examples-and-best-practices/`).
- "Call To Action" Buttons: Guidelines, Best Practices And Examples (`http://www.hongkiat.com/blog/call-to-action-buttons-guidelines-best-practices-and-examples/`).
- How To Design Call to Action Buttons That Convert (`http://unbounce.com/conversion-rate-optimization/design-call-to-action-buttons/`).

Normally, people need to get as much information as they can about the advantages and disadvantages before deciding to buy. So, under the header, we will display the list of items of the product or the key features offered.

In addition to the features list, we will also display customer testimonials within a slider. According to `www.entrepreneur.com` (`http://www.entrepreneur.com/article/83752`), displaying customer testimonials is one of the effective ways to drive more customers or sales, which is eventually good for business.

Below the testimonial section, the website will display the plan and price tables. And the last section will be the footer, containing secondary website navigation and links to Facebook and Twitter.

Let's now see how the website's layout will be in a smaller viewport size, which is as follows:

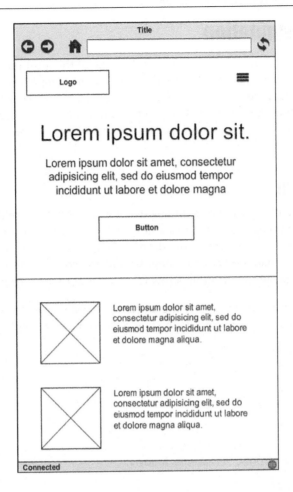

Much like the websites we built in the previous projects, all the content will be stacked. The catchphrases and the call-to-action button are aligned to the center. The menu in the navigation is now depicted as the hamburger icon. Next, we will see what Foundation has to offer in its package to build the website.

A look into Foundation

Foundation (`http://foundation.zurb.com/`) is one of the most popular frontend development frameworks. It is used by a number of notable companies, such as Pixar, Washington Post, Warby Parker (`https://www.warbyparker.com/`), and so on. As mentioned, Foundation ships with common web components and interactive widgets. Herein, we will look into the components, as well as the widgets we are going to employ for the website.

The grid system

The grid system is an integral part of a framework. It is one thing that makes managing web layout feel like a breeze. Foundation's grid system comprises twelve columns that can adapt to narrow viewport size through the drop-in classes provided. Similar to both the frameworks we explored in the previous chapters, the grid consists of rows and columns. Every column has to be wrapped within a row for the layout to span properly.

In Foundation, apply the `row` class to define an element as a row, and apply the element with the `columns` or `column` class to define it as a column. For example:

```
<div class="row">
<div class="columns">
</div>
<div class="columns">
</div>
</div>
```

You may also omit the *s* from `columns`, as follows:

```
<div class="row">
<div class="column">
</div>
<div class="column">
</div>
</div>
```

The column size is defined through the following series of classes:

- `small-{n}`: This specifies the grid column width in the small viewport size scope (approximately 0 px – 640 px).

- `medium-{n}`: This specifies the grid column width in the medium viewport size scope (approximately 641 px – 1,024 px).

- `large-{n}`: This specifies the grid column width in the large viewport size scope (approximately 1,025 px – 1,440 px).

> The {n} variable we gave in the preceding class names represents a number that spans from 1 to 12. The sum of the column number within a row should be no more than 12.

These classes can be applied in conjunction within a single element. For example:

```
<div class="row">
<div class="small-6 medium-4 columns"></div>
<div class="small-6 medium-8 columns"></div>
</div>
```

The preceding example gives the following result in the browser:

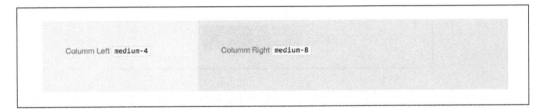

Resize the viewport size such that it is small enough and that the columns' width shifts following the assigned classes. In this case, each column has an equal width since both of them are assigned with the small-6 class:

> Generally, you may resize the viewport size by dragging the browser window. If you are using Chrome, you can activate the device mode and mobile emulator (https://developer.chrome.com/devtools/docs/device-mode). Or, if you use Firefox, you can enable the responsive design view (https://developer.mozilla.org/en-US/docs/Tools/Responsive_Design_View), which will allow you to resize the viewport size without having to drag the Firefox window.

The buttons

The button is essential for any kind of website, and we will certainly add a button in some places in the website. Foundation uses the button class to define an element as a button. You can assign the class to the elements, such as <a> and <button>. This class applies the default button styles, as shown in the following screenshot:

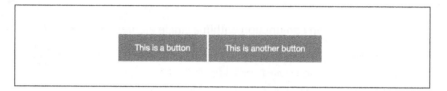

Furthermore, you can include additional classes to define the button color or context. Use one of the classes—secondary, success, alert—to set the button color:

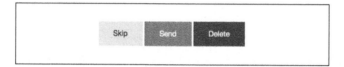

You can also specify the button size using one of the following classes: tiny, small, or large:

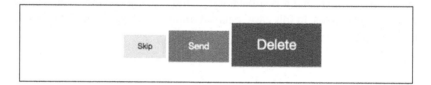

Make the button fancier with rounded corners using one of the classes, radius and round:

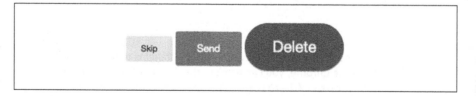

 There are a few more classes to form a button. Additionally, Foundation also provides multiple types of buttons, such as button groups, split buttons, and dropdown buttons. Hence, you may go to the **Buttons** section of the Foundation documents to find more about them.

The navigation and top bar

One of the important sections on a website is the navigation. The navigation helps users to browse the website from one page to another. Foundation, in this case, provides a couple of navigation types, and among them, one is called the top bar. Foundation's top bar will reside at the very top of the website before any content or section. The following is how the top bar will appear with the Foundation default style:

The top bar is responsive. Try resizing the browser's viewport size such that it is small enough, and you will find that the navigation is concealed within the menu, which requires us to click on **MENU** to reveal the full list of the menu items:

The Foundation top bar is primarily formed with the `top-bar` class to apply the styles, the `data-topbar` attribute to run the JavaScript function related to the top bar, and finally `role="navigation"` for better accessibility.

So, the following code is how we start to build the top bar in Foundation:

```
<nav class="top-bar" data-topbar role="navigation">
    ...
</nav>
```

Foundation splits the top bar content into two sections. The left-hand side area is called the title area, consisting of the website name or logo. Foundation constructs this section with the list element, as follows:

```
<ul class="title-area">
<li class="name">
    <h1><a href="#">Hello</a></h1>
  </li>
  <li class="toggle-topbar menu-icon">
<a href="#"><span>Menu</span></a>
</li>
</ul>
```

The second section is simply called the top bar section. Typically, this section contains the menu, buttons, and search form. Foundation sets this section using the `top-bar-section` class, along with the `left` and `right` class to specify the alignment. So, to put it all together, the following is the complete code to build a basic Foundation top bar, as you see in the preceding screenshots:

```
<nav class="top-bar" data-topbar role="navigation">
  <ul class="title-area">
    <li class="name">
      <h1><a href="#">Hello</a></h1>
    </li>
    <li class="toggle-topbar menu-icon">
<a href="#"><span>Menu</span></a>
</li>
  </ul>
<section class="top-bar-section">
    <ul class="right">
      <li class="active"><a href="#">Home</a></li>
      <li><a href="#">Blog</a></li>
      <li><a href="#">About</a></li>
      <li><a href="#">Contact</a></li>
    </ul>
  </section>
</nav>
```

Certainly, you will have to link the Foundation CSS style sheet beforehand in the document to see the top bar look.

The pricing tables

Whether you are selling products or services, you should name your price.

As we will build a website for business, we will need to display pricing tables. Fortunately, Foundation has included this component at its core, hence we won't need a third-party extension. For flexibility, Foundation structures a pricing table with the list element, as follows:

```
<ul class="pricing-table pricing-basic">
    <li class="title">Basic</li>
    <li class="price">$10<small>/month</small></li>
    <li class="description">Perfect for personal use.</li>
    <li class="bullet-item">1GB Storage</li>
    <li class="bullet-item">1 User</li>
    <li class="bullet-item">24/7 Support</li>
<li class="cta-button">
<a class="button success round" href="#">Sign Up</a>
</li>
</ul>
```

Each item in the list is set with a class, which I'm sure has explained itself through the name. Given the preceding HTML structure and the default style given through the Foundation CSS, the output turns out quite nicely, as shown in the following screenshot:

Moving around Orbit

The carousel or slider is one of the most popular design patterns on the web. Despite the debate with respect to its accessibility, many people still love to have it on their website— and so do we. Herein, we want to employ Orbit (http://foundation.zurb.com/docs/components/orbit.html), the Foundation jQuery plugin to display a content slider.

Orbit is customizable in that we can fully control the output, as well as the behavior of the slide through classes, attributes, or JavaScript initiation. We can also add almost anything within the Orbit slides, including textual content, images, links, and the mix. And needless to say, we can style most of its parts.

How is Orbit constructed?

Foundation uses the `list` element to construct the slide container, as well as the slides, and initiates the functionality using the HTML5 `data-` attribute named `data-orbit`. The following is a basic example of the Orbit slider structure, containing two slides of images:

```
<ul class="example-orbit" data-orbit>
<li><img src="image.jpg" alt="" /></li>
<li class="active"><img src="image2.jpg" alt="" /></li>
</ul>
```

Deploying Orbit is downright easy, and technically, it can contain almost any type of content within the slide and not only images. We will look more in that regard later as we build the website.

 For the time being, feel free to explore the Orbit slider section (http://foundation.zurb.com/docs/components/orbit.html) in Foundation's official website, which, to my account is the best place to get into the Orbit slider.

Adding add-ons, the font Icons

Foundation also provides a handful of add-ons, one of which is Webicons (http://zurb.com/playground/social-webicons). Needless to say, we will need social icons, and since these icons are basically vectors, they are infinitely scalable and thus will remain crisp and sharp in any screen resolution——normal or high definition. Have a look at the following icon set:

A few of the glyphs in the icon set

Aside from this icon set, you can also find the following:

◆ A collection of starter templates (http://foundation.zurb.com/templates.html) that will be useful to kick-off a new website and webpage

◆ Responsive tables (http://foundation.zurb.com/responsive-tables.html)

◆ Stencils (http://foundation.zurb.com/stencils.html), which you will find useful for sketching and prototyping new websites

Further on Foundation

Detailing every corner and aspect of Foundation is beyond the scope of this book. These are, by far, the most essential components of the framework that we are going to employ in the project and the website.

Fortunately, Packt Publishing has published a couple of titles that exclusively cover Foundation. I suggest you have a look at one of the following books if you are keen on further exploring the framework:

- *Learning Zurb Foundation, Kevin Horek, Packt Publishing* (https://www.packtpub.com/web-development/learning-zurb-foundation)

- *ZURB Foundation Blueprints, James Michael Stone, Packt Publishing* (https://www.packtpub.com/web-development/zurb-foundation-blueprints)

Additional required assets

There are several files that we will need in addition to Foundation's own components. These files encompass the image cover for the website header, the icons that will represent the feature in the website feature list section, the favicon image as well as the Apple icons, the avatar image to display in the testimonial section, and finally (which is also important) the website logo.

In terms of the header image, we will use the following image photographed by Alejandro Escamilla, which shows a man working with his Macbook Air; the screen seems off though (http://unsplash.com/post/51493972685/download-by-alejandro-escamilla):

The icons to display alongside the feature list items are designed by Nick Frost from Ballicons (`http://ballicons.net/`). Among the icons in the collection that we will include in the website are the following:

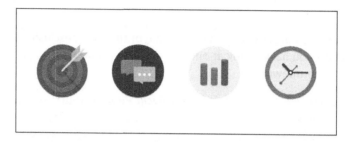

The following are the favicon and the Apple icon, which are generated using a Photoshop action called AppIconTemplate (`http://appicontemplate.com/`):

Favicon and the Apple icon

We will use the mystery man of WordPress as the default avatar. This avatar image will be displayed above the testimonial lines, as shown in the following wireframe:

The mystery man

The logo of this website is made with SVG for the sake of clarity and scalability. The logo is shown in the following screenshot:

You can get all these assets from the source files that come along with this book. Otherwise, grab them from the URL that we showed in the preceding paragraphs.

The project directories, assets, and dependencies

Once we assess the website layout, the framework features, and all the assets required, we will start working on the project. Herein, we will start getting the project directories and the assets organized. Also, we will grab and record all the project dependencies through Bower, the second project with Bootstrap. So, it's time for action.

Time for action – organizing the project directories, assets, and dependencies

1. In the `htdocs` folder, create a new folder, and name it `startup`. This is the folder in which the website will live.

2. Within the `startup` folder, create a folder named `assets` to contain all the assets like the style sheets, JavaScripts, images, and others.

3. Inside the `assets` folder create folders to group these assets:

    ❑   `css` for the style sheets.

    ❑   `js` to contain the JavaScripts.

    ❑   `scss` to contain SCSS style sheet (more about SCSS in the next chapter).

    ❑   `img` to contain the images.

    ❑   `fonts` to contain the font icons.

4. Add the images, including the website logo, header image, icons, and the avatar image, as shown in the following screenshot:

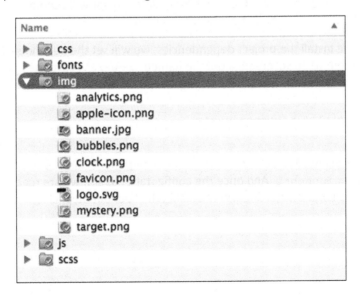

5. Now, we will download the project dependencies, which will include the Foundation framework, the icons, jQuery, and a couple of other libraries. Hence, let's open a terminal or command prompt if you are using Windows. Then, navigate to the project directory with the `cd` command:

   ❑ In Windows: `cd \xampp\htdocs\startup`

   ❑ In OSX: `cd /Applications/XAMPP/htdocs/startup`

   ❑ In Ubuntu: `cd /opt/lampp/htdocs/startup`

6. As we did in the second project, type the command, fill out the prompts to set the project specification, including the project name and the project version, as shown in the following screenshot:

```
  ● ○ ○
→  startup git:(terminal)    bower init
[?] name: startup
[?] version: 1.0.0
[?] description: An example of corporate website built
[?] main file: index.html
[?] what types of modules does this package expose? global
[?] keywords: startup, responsive, foundation
[?] authors: Thoriq Firdaus <tfirdaus@creatiface.com>
[?] license: MIT
[?] homepage: https://github.com/tfirdaus/rwd-startup
[?] set currently installed components as dependencies?
[?] add commonly ignored files to ignore list? Yes
[?] would you like to mark this package as private which
```

When all the prompts are filled and completed, Bower will generate a new file named `bower.json` to put all the information in.

7. Before we install the project dependencies, we will set the dependencies folder destination. To do so, create a dot file named `.bowerrc`. Save the file with the following lines in it:

```
{
   "directory": "components"
}
```

This line will tell Bower to name the folder components instead of `bower_components`. And once the configuration is set, we are ready to install the libraries, starting with installing the Foundation package.

8. To install the Foundation package through Bower, type `bower install foundation --save`. Make sure that the `--save` parameter is included to record Foundation within the `bower.json file`.

> Apart from the Foundation primary package (files like the style sheet and JavaScript), this command will also grab libraries that are associated with Foundation, namely:
>
> Fastclick (`https://github.com/ftlabs/fastclick`)
>
> jQuery (`http://jquery.com/`)
>
> jQuery Cookie (`https://github.com/carhartl/jquery-cookie`)
>
> jQuery Placeholder (`https://github.com/mathiasbynens/jquery-placeholder`)
>
> Modernizr (`http://modernizr.com/`)

9. The Foundation font icon is set in a separate repository. To install it, type the `bower install foundation-icons --save` command.

10. The Foundation icon package comes with the style sheet that specifies and presents the icon through HTML classes and also the icon files. Herein, we need to make a copy of the font from the package folder into our own `fonts` folder. Have a look at the following screenshot:

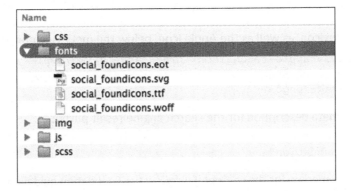

What just happened?

We just created the project directory, as well as folders to organize the project assets. In addition, we also installed the libraries that are required to build the website through Bower, which include the Foundation framework.

Having added in the images and the libraries, we will build the website's home page markup in the next section. So, without further ado, let's move on, and it's time for action again.

Time for action – building the website's HTML structure

1. Create a new HTML file named `index.html`. Then, open it in Sublime Text, our code editor of choice in this book.

2. Let's add the basic HTML5 structure as follows:

```
<!DOCTYPE html>
<html lang="en">
<head>
  <meta charset="UTF-8">
  <title>Startup</title>
</head>
<body>

</body>
</html>
```

3. Add the meta `X-UA-Compatible` variable with the content value `IE=edge` to allow Internet Explorer to use its latest cutting-edge rendering version:

```
<meta http-equiv="X-UA-Compatible" content="IE=edge">
```

4. Not to forget the meta `viewport` tag required to make the website responsive; add it in `<head>` as follows:

```
<meta name="viewport" content="width=device-width, initial-scale=1">
```

5. Add the favicon, as well as the Apple icon, below the meta viewport tag, as follows:

```
<link rel="apple-touch-icon" href="assets/img/apple-icon.png">
<link rel="shortcut icon" href="assets/img/favicon.png" type="image/png">
```

6. Add the meta description for the search engine result purposes:

```
<meta name="description" content="A startup company website built using Foundation">
```

7. The HTML markup for the content will follow the Foundation guidelines, as we have discussed in the early sections of this book. In addition, we may add extra classes in the elements to customize the styles. Let's start off by adding the website `<header>`, for which, add the following lines within `<body>`:

```
<header class="startup-header">
...
</header>
```

8. Next, add the website navigation bar within the header, as follows:

```
<header class="startup-header">
<div class="contain-to-grid startup-top-bar">
<nav class="top-bar" data-topbar>
    <ul class="title-area">
        <li class="name startup-name">
            <h1><a href="#">Startup</a></h1>
        </li>
<li class="toggle-topbar menu-icon">
        <a href="#"><span>Menu</span></a>
</li>
</ul>
        <section class="top-bar-section">
          <ul class="right">
            <li><a href="#">Features</a></li>
<li><a href="#">Pricing</a></li>
<li><a href="#">Blog</a></li>
<li class="has-form log-in"><a href="" class="button secondary
round">Log In</a></li>
<li class="has-form sign-up"><a href="#" class="button round">Sign
Up</a></li>
            </ul>
</section>
</nav>
</div>
</header>
```

9. Below the navigation bar HTML markup, we add the catchphrase and call-to-action button, as follows:

```
<header class="startup-header">
  . . .
<div class="panel startup-hero">
      <div class="row">
<h2 class="hero-title">Stay Cool and be Awesome</h2>
<p class="hero-lead">The most awesome web application in the
galaxy.</p>
</div>
      <div class="row">
<a href="#" class="button success round">Signup</a>
      </div>
</div>
</header>
```

10. Next, we will add the website's body content that will contain the product feature list section, the testimonial section, and the plan table price. First, add a `<div>` that will wrap the body content sections below the header, as follows:

```
<div class="startup-body">
...
</div>
```

11. Within `<div>`, we add the HTML markup for the feature list section, as follows:

```
<div class="startup-body">
<div class="startup-features">
<div class="row">
    <div class="medium-6 columns">
        <div class="row">
            <div class="small-3 medium-4 columns">
            <figure>
<img src="assets/img/analytics.png" height="128" width="128"
alt="">
            </figure>
</div>
        <div class="small-9 medium-8 columns">
          <h4>Easy</h4>
<p>This web application is super easy to use. No complicated
setup. It just works out of the box.</p>
 </div>
        </div>
        </div>
        <div class="medium-6 columns">
          <div class="row">
<div class="small-3 medium-4 columns">
            <figure>
            <img src="assets/img/clock.png" height="128"
width="128" alt="">
            </figure>
          </div>
          <div class="small-9 medium-8 columns">
            <h4>Fast</h4>
            <p>This web application runs in a
blink of eye. There is no other application that is on par with
our application in term of speed.</p>
            </div>
          </div>
        </div>
      </div>
      <div class="row">
        <div class="medium-6 columns">
          <div class="row">
<div class="small-3 medium-4 columns">
            <figure>
```

```
    <img src="assets/img/target.png" height="128" width="128" alt="">
</figure>
                        </div>
<div class="small-9 medium-8 columns">
    <h4>Secure</h4>
<p>Your data is encyrpted with the latest Kryptonian technology.
It will never be shared to anyone. Rest assured, your data is
totally safe.</p>
                        </div>
                    </div>
                </div>
                <div class="medium-6 columns">
                    <div class="row">
                        <div class="small-3 medium-4 columns">
                            <figure>
                                <img src="assets/img/bubbles.png"
height="128" width="128" alt="">
                            </figure>
                        </div>
                        <div class="small-9 medium-8 columns">
                            <h4>Awesome</h4>
                            <p>It's simply the most awesome web
application and make you the coolest person in the galaxy. Enough
said.</p>
                        </div>
                    </div>
                </div>
            </div>
        </div>
    </div>
</div>
```

The column division for this section refers to the layout shown in the website
wireframe. So, as you can see from the preceding code that we just added, each
feature list item is assigned with medium-6 columns, hence the column width of
each item will be equal.

12. Below the feature list section, we add the testimonial section's HTML markup,
as follows:

```
<div class="startup-body">
...
<div class="startup-testimonial">
        <div class="row">
            <ul class="testimonial-list" data-orbit>
                <li data-orbit-slide="testimonial-1">
                    <div>
                        <blockquote>Lorem ipsum dolor sit
amet, consectetur adipisicing elit. Dolor numquam quaerat
doloremque in quis dolore enim modi cumque eligendi eius.</
blockquote>
```

```
                    <figure>
                        <img class="avatar" src="assets/
img/mystery.png" height="128" width="128" alt="">
                        <figcaption>John Doe</figcaption>
                    </figure>
                </div>
            </li>
            <li data-orbit-slide="testimonial-2">
                <div>
                    <blockquote>Lorem ipsum dolor sit
amet, consectetur adipisicing elit.</blockquote>
                    <figure>
                        <img class="avatar" src="assets/
img/mystery.png" height="128" width="128" alt="">
                        <figcaption>Jane Doe</figcaption>
                    </figure>
                </div>
            </li>
        </ul>
    </div>
  </div>
</div>
```

13. Referring to the layout in the wireframe, we should add the plan price table below the testimonial section, as follows:

```
<div class="startup-body">
<!-- ... feature list section … -->
<!-- ... testimonial section … -->
<div class="startup-pricing">
        <div class="row">
            <div class="medium-4 columns">
                <ul class="pricing-table pricing-basic">
                    <li class="title">Basic</li>
                    <li class="price">$10<small>/month</
small></li>
                    <li class="description">Perfect for
personal use.</li>
                    <li class="bullet-item">1GB Storage</li>
                    <li class="bullet-item">1 User</li>
                    <li class="bullet-item">24/7 Support</li>
                    <li class="cta-button"><a class="button
success round" href="#">Sign Up</a></li>
                </ul>
            </div>
            <div class="medium-4 columns">
                <ul class="pricing-table pricing-team">
                    <li class="title">Team</li>
                    <li class="price">$50<small>/month</
small></li>
```

```
                          <li class="description">For a small
team.</li>
                          <li class="bullet-item">50GB Storage</li>
                          <li class="bullet-item">Up to 10 Users</
li>
                          <li class="bullet-item">24/7 Support</li>
                          <li class="cta-button"><a class="button
success round" href="#">Sign Up</a></li>
                      </ul>
                  </div>
                  <div class="medium-4 columns">
                      <ul class="pricing-table pricing-enterprise">
                          <li class="title">Enterprise</li>
                          <li class="price">$300<small>/month</
small></li>
                          <li class="description">For large
corporation</li>
                          <li class="bullet-item">Unlimited
Storage</li>
                          <li class="bullet-item">Unlimited Users</
li>
                          <li class="bullet-item">24/7 Priority
Support</li>
                          <li class="cta-button"><a class="button
success round" href="#">Sign Up</a></li>
                      </ul>
                  </div>
              </div>
          </div>
      </div>
```

14. Finally, we add the website footer below the body content, as follows:

```
</div> <!—the body content end -->
<footer class="startup-footer">
      <div class="row footer-nav">
          <ul class="secondary-nav">
              <li><a href="#">About</a></li>
              <li><a href="#">Contact</a></li>
              <li><a href="#">Help</a></li>
              <li><a href="#">Careers</a></li>
              <li><a href="#">Terms</a></li>
              <li><a href="#">Privacy</a></li>
          </ul>
          <ul class="social-nav">
              <li><a class="foundicon-facebook"
href="#">Facebook</a></li>
              <li><a class="foundicon-twitter"
href="#">Twitter</a></li>
          </ul>
```

```
        </div>
        <div class="row footer-copyright">
             <p>Copyright 2014 Super Awesome App. All rights
reserved.</p>
        </div>
    </footer>
</body>
```

What just happened?

We just built the HTML markup for the website content and sections by following the Foundation guidelines. We also added extra classes along the way to customize the Foundation default styles later on.

Since building the HTML markup, we haven't added any of the styles; the website, at this point, looks white and plain, as shown in the following screenshot:

- **Startup**
  - Menu
  - Features
  - Pricing
  - Blog
  - Log In
  - Sign Up

Stay Cool and be Awesome

The most awesome web application in the galaxy.

Signup

Easy

This web application is super easy to use. No complicated setup. It just works out of the box.

Fast

This web application runs in a blink of eye. There is no other application that is on par with our application in term of speed.

Secure

Your data is encyrpted with the latest Kryptonian technology. It will never be shared to anyone. Rest assured, your data is totally safe.

Awesome

The full code of the HTML that we have just added can also be found at `http://git.io/qvdupQ`.

Summary

This chapter effectively started off our third project. In this project, we use Foundation to build a website for a start-up company. We walked through the Foundation features and adopted some of them into the website. We only added the website's HTML structure in this chapter though. The website, at this point, still looks plain and white. We have to compose the styles to define what the website looks and feels like, which is exactly what we will do in the next chapter.

We will compose the website styles using Sass, the CSS preprocessor that also defined the Foundation basic styles. Hence, at the beginning of the next chapter, first, we will learn to use Sass variable, mixins, functions, and other Sass features before we write the website styles.

It looks like there is still a lot of work left to do in order to accomplish this project. So, without further ado, let's move on to the next chapter.

8
Extending Foundation

After constructing the website page markup in the previous chapter, we now start giving the website a look, feel, and colors. This time we will use **Sassy CSS (SCSS)**, *which also happens to be the underlying syntax of the Foundation default styles.*

SCSS is a syntax variation of a CSS preprocessor named Sass. The Sass original syntax uses indentation formatting that makes the codes look neat. SCSS, on the other hand, uses curly braces and semicolons just like regular CSS. The similarity helps everyone to quickly grasp the syntax, in particular those who are new to Sass.

Since we are going to employ SCSS, we will start off this chapter by walking you through a couple of Sass features and its utilities. You will learn to define variables and functions, perform operations, and comply with other directives, which allows us to compose the website style rules more efficiently.

This might sound challenging. And if you like a challenge, we can just get started right away.

This chapter will revolve around the following topics:

♦ Exploring Sass features and learning the syntax

♦ Looking into Bourbon, a Sass mixins library

♦ Organizing the style sheet structure and using the Import directive to include partial style sheets

♦ Setting up Koala to compile SCSS into CSS

- Customizing Foundation's default styles through variables
- Composing the website custom styles
- Optimizing the website layout for various viewport sizes
- Turning the website live by compiling the JavaScripts

Syntactically Awesome Style Sheets

Sass (http://sass-lang.com/) is a CSS preprocessor created by Hampton Catlin, Natalie Weizenbaum, and Chris Eppstein, which is the same team that also created Haml (http://haml.info/). Foundation, as mentioned at the beginning of this chapter, uses Sass to generate its CSS, and so will we. So, before we get our hands dirty, first we will delve into several Sass features, such as nesting, variables, mixins, functions, and others, that will allow us to write style rules more efficiently.

Nesting rules

Sass allows us to nest style rules into one another. This feature eventually allows us to write style rules that resemble the HTML structure of the web page. That way, the style rules can be more concise and more easy to scan through. Say, we added the header markup of our website, as follows:

```
<header>
  <h1><a href="#">Website</a></h1>
</header>
```

With Sass, we can construct the style rules, as follows:

```
header {
  background: #000;
  h1 {
    margin: 0;
    a {
      color: #fff;
    }
  }
}
```

It's worth noticing that even though Sass allows you to nest style rules, you should not abuse this facility. So, don't do something like the following code:

```
body {
  nav {
    ul {
      li {
        a {
          &:before {


          }
        }
      }
    }
  }
}
```

Consider it before nesting style rules. The main objective of this feature is to make the style rules look simpler, more concise, easier to scan through, and not to make it unnecessarily look more complex.

Storing a value with a variable

A variable is one useful piece in programming language that allows us to define a value once within a specified name. Each language has a slightly different way to declare a variable. For example, JavaScript uses the keyword `var`, LESS uses @, and Sass in this case uses the $ sign.

One of the perfectly-suited implementations of a variable is to define the website colors, for example:

```
$primary: #000;
$secondary: #bdc3c7;
$tertiary: #2ecc71;
$quaternary: #2980b9;
$quinary: #e67e22;
```

So, instead of declaring the color value every time we need it, we can simply declare the representative variables. In the following example, we declare $primary as the body text color and $secondary as the background color:

```
body {
  background-color: $secondary;
  color: $primary;
}
```

When compiled to regular CSS, these variables are replaced with the defined value, as follows:

```
body {
  background-color: #bdc3c7;
  color: #000;
}
```

Using a variable with a proper name (of course), you will find it easier to write the variable rather than remembering the Hex or the RGB number; well, it is practically easier to write $primary than #bdc3c7, isn't it?

The Sass variable isn't exclusively aimed to define colors. We can also use a variable to define a string or plain text, as follows:

```
$var: "Hello World";
$body-font-family: "Helvetica Neue";
```

We can use a variable to store a number or a length:

```
$number: 9;
$global-radius: 3px;
```

We can use a variable to inherit the value of another variable:

```
$var: $anotherVar;
$header-font-family: $body-font-family;
```

We can use a variable to define the output of a function:

```
$h1-font-size: rem-calc(44);
```

Foundation centralized the declaration of its primary variables within a file named _settings.scss. We will look more into this matter later when we compose the website style rules.

Variable interpolation

There are certain circumstances when a variable is not applicable, such as when it is inserted within a string (plain text), as follows:

```
$var: "Hello";
$newVar: "$var World";
div {
  content: $newVar;
}
```

When compiled, the `$var` declaration within `$newVar` won't be replaced with the value of `"Hello"`. This is because Sass interprets `$var` as a string or plain text. Thus, the output of the following example will simply be:

```
div {
  content: "$var World";
}
```

Another example where a variable won't work is when a declaration is begun with an `@` rule or a directive, as follows:

```
$screen-size: (max-width: 600px);
@media $screen-size {
  div {
    display: none;
  }
}
```

This example simply returns an error to the Sass compiler because `@media` is supposed to be followed by either the `print` or `screen` keyword.

There are a few cases where we have to use interpolation to declare a variable. Variable interpolation happens to other programming languages, such as PHP, Ruby, and Swift. But I'm not going into the details of the technicalities of its workings, as I don't exactly know either. Simply put, interpolation allows us to embed a variable in a situation where it does not allow the variable to work—especially where it is a string that is actually expected.

Each programming language has its notation to enable interpolation. In this case, Sass uses `#{}`. Given one of the previous examples, we can write the variable as follows:

```
$var: "Hello";
$newVar: "#{$var} World";
div {
  content: $newVar;
}
```

And the result will be as follows:

```
div {
  content: "Hello World";
}
```

Follow Hugo Giraudel posts (`https://webdesign.tutsplus.com/tutorials/all-you-ever-need-to-know-about-sass-interpolation--cms-21375`) for further assistance about variable interpolation in Sass.

Reusable code block with mixins

Now, we are going to look into Sass mixins. If you followed and accomplished the second project, you should know about LESS mixins. Mixins, both in Sass and LESS, have similar purposes; they allow developers to reuse code blocks and style rules within the entire style sheet and thus comply with the DRY principle (http://programmer.97things. oreilly.com/wiki/index.php/Don't_Repeat_Yourself). However, it is slightly different in terms of how we declare and reuse the mixins. This is how we declare a mixin in LESS:

```less
.buttons {
  color: @link-color;
  font-weight: normal;
  border-radius: 0;
}
```

In Sass, we use the `@mixins` directive to create a mixin, for example:

```scss
$linkColor: $tertiary;
@mixin buttons {
  color: $linkColor;
  font-weight: normal;
  border-radius: 0;
}
```

Sass uses the `@include` directive to reuse the preceding code block within style rules. Given the preceding example, we can write:

```scss
.button {
  @include buttons;
}
```

The following is the output when the preceding example is compiled to CSS:

```css
.button {
  color: #2ecc71;
  font-weight: normal;
  border-radius: 0;
}
```

That is a basic example of the application of Sass mixins.

A brief on the Sass mixin library

Some CSS3 syntaxes are so complex that writing them can be really tedious work. And this is where mixins can be particularly useful. Fortunately, with Sass being so popular and supported by so many generous developers, we don't have to port all CSS3 syntax into Sass mixins on our own. Instead, we can simply employ Sass's mixin library that makes our work as a web developer more enjoyable.

The Sass library comes with a collection of useful mixins and functions (we will talk about functions shortly) that we can use right away out-of-the-box. There are dozens of popular libraries available, and one that we are going to use herein is called Bourbon (`http://bourbon.io/`).

Bourbon compiles a number of mixins in a library that simplifies the way we declare CSS3 syntax, including syntax that is still marked as experimental, such as `image-rendering`, `filter`, and the CSS3 `calc` function. Now, which do you think is easier and faster to write when it comes to specifying the Hi-DPI Media Query?

 Hi-DPI Media Query is used to measure the device pixel density, for which we can use it to deliver higher-resolution graphics on web pages, specifically on devices with hi-definition screens. The following are some references for further information on the subject:

- High DPI Images for Variable Pixel Densities by Boris Smus (`http://www.html5rocks.com/en/mobile/high-dpi/`).
- Towards A Retina Web by Reda Lemeden (`http://www.smashingmagazine.com/2012/08/20/towards-retina-web/`).

Is the following standard syntax?

```
@media only screen and (-webkit-min-device-pixel-ratio: 2),
only screen and (min--moz-device-pixel-ratio: 2),
only screen and (-o-min-device-pixel-ratio: 2 / 1),
only screen and (min-resolution: 192dpi),
only screen and (min-resolution: 2dppx) {
  width: 500px;
}
```

Or, will it be the following one with the Bourbon mixin?:

```
@include hidpi(2) {
  width: 500px;
}
```

Without spending years researching, we can commonly agree that using the mixin should be a lot easier to write, as well as easier to remember.

> As mentioned, in addition to CSS3 mixins, Bourbon also ships with a couple of Sass functions, such as Triangle, which allows us to create CSS-based triangles. However, I'm not going to mention all the bits that are there in the Bourbon library. Since the library collection will most likely be updated or revised along with the introduction of new CSS specifications, it is better to refer to the list on the official documentation page (http://bourbon.io/docs/).

Creating and using a Sass function

A function is one piece of a feature that makes creating style rules more dynamic. A function in Sass is declared using the @function directive, which is then followed by the function name, a parameter with preferably its default value. In its simplest form, a Sass function may look as follows:

```
@function color($parameter: green) {

}
```

This function, however, won't output anything yet. To generate a result of this function, we need to add a @return value. Given the preceding example, we want to output the default value parameter, which says "hello". To do so, we write the @return value, which is then followed by $parameter, as follows:

```
@function color($parameter: green) {
  @return $parameter;
}
```

Use this function within a selector, as follows:

```
@function name($parameter: green) {
  @return $parameter;
}
.selector {
  color: name();
}
```

Compile it, and you get the following output:

```
.selector {
  color: green;
}
```

Customize the output by specifying a new value out of the default one, as follows:

```
.selector {
  color: name(yellow);
}
```

We will get a new output, as shown in the following code:

```
.selector {
  color: yellow;
}
```

> This example merely shows the basic functionality of a function. There are a lot more examples on how we can utilize it in real cases to build reusable code series. So, I recommend you head over to the following references for further advanced discussion and find more examples.
>
> Using pure Sass functions to make reusable logic more useful (http:// thesassway.com/advanced/pure-sass-functions).
>
> A couple of Sass functions (http://hugogiraudel.com/2013/08/12/ sass-functions/).

Manipulating color with Sass functions

One thing that I love about using CSS preprocessors such as Sass, is how easy it is to determine and alter colors. Sass, in this case, provides a bunch of built-in functions to manipulate colors seamlessly. The following is a list of a few Sass color functions for your reference, which may be useful to manipulate colors in the website later on:

Functions	Description	Example

`lighten($color, $amount)`	Turns a color lighter by the specified amount.	`$black: #000000`
		`lighten($black, 10%);`
		In this example, we lighten `$black` by 10 percent. The output is #1a1a1a.

`darken($color, $amount)`	Turns a color darker than the specified amount.	`$white: #ffffff;`
		`darken($white, 10%)`
		In this example, we darken `$white` by 10 percent. The output will be #e6e6e6.

Functions	Description	Example

`fade-out ($color, $amount)`	Turns the color to be more transparent than the specified amount.	`$black: #000000;`
		
		`fade-out ($black, .5);`
		
		In this example, we change the `$black` color to be compiled into RGB format and set the transparency to 50 percent. The output is `rgba (0, 0, 0, 0.5)`.

> Please follow the Sass official documentation (`http://sass-lang.com/documentation/Sass/Script/Functions.html`) to find out the full list of the color functions available.

Useful Foundation's own function

The Foundation framework comes with an array of its own functions. Foundation uses these functions to build its own default styles, and we can also use them to build our own. One such useful function therein is `rem-calc()`, which allows us to calculate the `rem` unit with less hassle.

Em and Rem

The `rem` unit is a relative value that inherited concepts similar to em. Here is what Ian Yates expounded about the origin of em in his post (`https://webdesign.tutsplus.com/articles/taking-the-erm-out-of-ems--webdesign-12321`):

> *"Ems get their name from printing. Precisely when the term was first used is unclear, but as the uppercase M (pronounced emm) most closely represents the square printing block on which printing letters were placed, it came to lend its name to the measurement. Whatever the point size of the font in question, the block of the uppercase M would define the Em."*

But the problem with the em unit, as Jonathan Snook described in his post (`http://snook.ca/archives/html_and_css/font-size-with-rem`), is its compounding nature. Since the size is relative to its closest parent, in my experience the size output can be unpredictably frustrating at best; the size will be varying depending on where it is specified. Examine the following example:

```
body {
    font-size:16px;
}
div {
```

```
        font-size: 1.2em; /* 19px */
}
ul {
        font-size: 1em; /* 19px */
}
ul li {
        font-size: 1.2em; /* 23px */
}
```

This is where the `rem` unit comes in. The `rem` unit measures the calculation directly against the font size of `<html>`, the root element of an HTML document—thus, it is also dubbed as root `em`. Regardless of where the unit is specified, the result will be precise, consistent, and more importantly, easy to figure out (it's like the `px` unit, but it's relative).

The `rem-calc` function accepts both integer and length. Hence, the following code examples work:

```
div {
   font-size: rem-calc(12);
}
span {
   font-size: rem-calc(10px);
}
p {
   font-size: rem-calc(11em);
}
```

In this case, they will turn out to be as follows:

```
div {
   font-size: 0.75rem;
}
span {
   font-size: 0.625rem;
}
p {
   font-size: 0.6875rem;
}
```

Have a go hero – diving into Sass

There is a lot more about Sass than we are able to cover in this book, such as placeholder, conditional statement, and operators, just to name a few. Thankfully, there are enough good references and books that have covered Sass, as well as its supporting utilities in greater depth, into which you can dig into on your own. The following are some of my best recommendations:

- *Sass and Compass for Designers, Ben Frain, Packt Publishing* (https://www. packtpub.com/web-development/sass-and-compass-designers)
- *Sass for Web Designers, Dan Cederholm, A Book Apart* (http://www. abookapart.com/products/sass-for-web-designers)
- The Sass Way—tutorials and tips on using Sass (http://thesassway.com/)
- A dedicated category on web design tutorials and for covering anything related to Sass (https://webdesign.tutsplus.com/categories/sass)

Before we resume the work, let's end this section with a couple of quizzes, shall we?

Pop quiz – multiple parameters in Sass function

In the preceding section, we discussed about Sass function, as well as showed you the simplest example out of it. In the example, we created a function with only one parameter. The fact is that we can add multiple parameters within a single Sass function.

Q1. So, which among the following examples is the correct way to create a function with multiple parameters?

1. Each parameter is separated with a semicolon.

   ```
   @function name($a:1px; $b:2px){
   @return $a + $b
   }
   ```

2. Each parameter is separated with an addition operator.

   ```
   @function name($a:2px + $b:2px){
   @return $a + $b
   }
   ```

3. Each parameter is separated with a comma.

   ```
   @function name($a:1px, $b:2px){
   @return $a + $b
   }
   ```

Pop quiz – Sass color manipulation

Q1. There are lots of Sass functions built-in. In this section, we named three, `lighten()`, `darken()`, and `fade-out()`, which I think are sufficient to help us to decorate the website of this project. The `fade-out()` function has an alias that also gives us the same result. So, which of the following is the name alias for the fade-out() function?

1. `transparentize($color, $amount)`

2. `transparency($color, $amount)`

3. `transparent($color, $amount)`

Project recap

In *Chapter 7, A Responsive Website for Business with Foundation*, we installed Foundation and Foundation Icons, along with their dependencies (jQuery, Fastclick, Modernizr, and so on) through Bower (`http://bower.io/`). We also prepared the website assets, namely, the images, image icons, and the website logo. In the last section of the chapter, we created `index.html` for the website home page, and we also constructed the markup using a couple of new HTML5 tags. So, the files and folders that are currently in the working directory are shown in the following screenshot:

Style sheet organizations

Files that are still missing from our working directories are the style sheets to compose our customized styles for the website, and the Bourbon library that we briefly mentioned in the preceding section to provide us with some ready-to-use mixins and functions. This is what we are going to do in this section. We are going to create style sheets and organize them in a way to make them easily maintainable in the future.

Well, let's resume the work.

Time for action – organizing and compiling style sheets

Perform the following steps right to the end to properly organize the style sheets and compile them into CSS.

1. We need to install Bourbon. Launch a terminal or the command prompt, and type the following command:

```
bower install bourbon --save
```

This command installs the Bourbon package through the Bower registry and registers it within the `bower.json` file of the project.

I've discussed the `bower.json` file exclusively in this post (`https://webdesign.tutsplus.com/tutorials/quick-tip-what-to-do-when-you-encounter-a-bower-file--cms-21162`), check it out!

2. Create new style sheets named `main.scss`, `responsive.scss`, and `styles.scss` in the `scss` folder.

3. The `_main.scss` style sheet is the one where we will put all our own style rules. We will use the `_responsive.scss` file to exclusively put in the media queries of the website. And the `styles.scss` file is where we will compile those style sheets together.

The underscore _ that began the file name is a special notation that tells the Sass compiler not to directly compile the file.

4. Still within the `scss` folder, create two more style sheets. This time, name them `_config.scss` and `foundation.scss`.

5. The `_config.scss` will contain a copy of all the variables used in Foundation, while `foundation.scss` will contain imported partials of Foundation style sheets. These copies will prevent us from directly modifying the original files, which will eventually be overridden when we update to the newest version.

6. Next, copy the whole content of the Foundation `_settings.scss` file to the `_config.scss` file that we recently created. In our case, the `_settings.scss` file is located in the `/components/foundation/scss/foundation/` directory.

7. Also, copy the whole content of Foundation's own `foundation.scss` and paste it to our own `foundation.scss` that we also recently created.

8. Then, we need to correct the path of the imported partials in our `foundation.scss` file. At this stage, all paths are pointing to the `foundation` folder, as follows:

```
@import "foundation/components/grid";
@import "foundation/components/accordion";
@import "foundation/components/alert-boxes";
... /* other imports */
```

This certainly is incorrect because we don't have a folder named `foundation` in the `scss` folder. Herein, we need to direct the path to the `components` folder instead, where the partials actually reside. So, change the path to be as follows:

```
@import "../../components/foundation/scss/foundation/components/
grid";
@import "../../components/foundation/scss/foundation/components/
accordion";
@import "../../components/foundation/scss/foundation/components/
alert-boxes";
... /* other imports */
```

 A comprehensive snippet of Foundation partial references can be found in the Gist (`http://git.io/1dITag`).

 In Sass, we don't have to specify the `.scss` or `.sass` extension when it comes to importing external files. The Sass compiler is clever enough to determine the extension on its own. And this is also because a plain CSS is also a valid Sass.

9. Another path that we have to correct is the path referring to the Foundation, `_functions.scss`, which contains the `rem-calc()` function. Open the `_config.scss` file, and change the line `@import "foundation/functions";` to `@import "../../components/foundation/scss/foundation/functions";`.

10. We are going to compile these style sheets into CSS using Koala. Launch Koala and add the working directory:

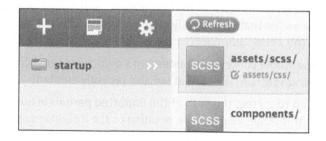

11. Within the style list in Koala, you won't find the SCSS style sheets with the underscore prefix. Koala, by default, ignores this file since it eventually won't be compiled into CSS.

12. However, you should find the two primary style sheets of the project listed therein, namely, `styles.scss` and `foundation.scss`. Be sure that this output is set to the `css` folder, as shown in the following screenshot:

13. Then, make sure that the option of `Auto Compile` is checked so that they will be automatically compiled into CSS, as we've made changes. Also, check the `Source Map` option to make debugging the style sheet easier. Have a look at the following screenshot:

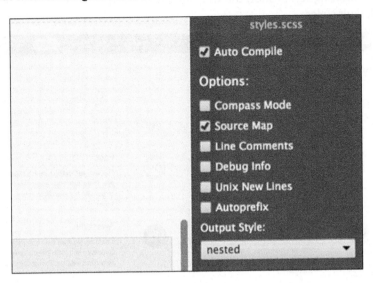

14. Click the **Compile** button of `styles.scss` and `foundation.scss` to compile them into CSS.

15. Open `index.html` and link both the compiled CSSs within the `<head>` tag, as follows:

```
<link rel="stylesheet" href="assets/css/foundation.css">
<link rel="stylesheet" href="assets/css/styles.css">
```

What just happened?

We just installed Bourbon and put together several new style sheets to style the website. Then, we compiled them into CSS, and then linked them to `index.html`. Hence, as you can see in the following screenshot, the website is now starting to take place—with the Foundation default styles:

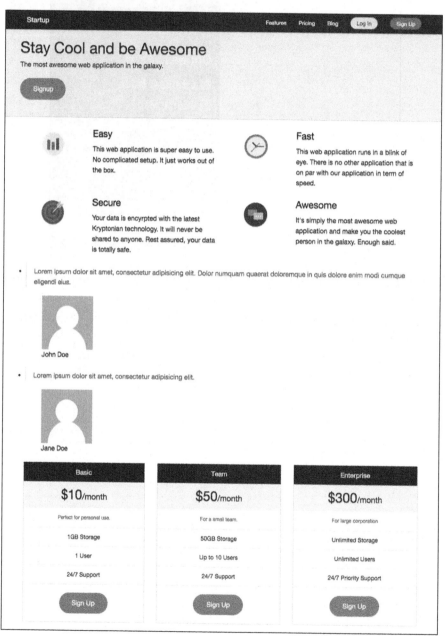

The website's look and feel

With the style sheets organized and compiled, now comes the time to customize the website's styles. As it happens, we don't have to write every bit of the style rules on our own. In this case, since we are using a framework (Foundation), sometimes customizing the website styles can be as easy as changing the default value in a variable.

Without further ado, let's move on.

Time for action – build on the website

Styling the website will involve multiple style sheets. Hence, follow the following steps carefully:

1. Import the following style sheets in `foundation.scss`:

   ```
   @import "config";
   @import "../../components/foundation/scss/normalize";
   @import "../../components/foundation-icons/foundation_icons_
   social/sass/social_foundicons.scss";
   ... /* other partials */
   ```

   That way, the variables, as well as the changes within `_config.scss`, will affect other component style sheets through Foundation. The `normalize` variable will standardize basic element styles, `social_foundicons.scss`; as you can guess, this allows us to apply Foundation's social icons.

2. Open `styles.scss` and import Bourbon, `_config.scss`, `main.scss`, and `responsive.scss`, as follows:

   ```
   @import "../../components/bourbon/dist/bourbon";
   @import "config";
   @import "main";
   @import "responsive";
   ```

3. Then, I want to apply a custom font from Google Font simply because the custom fonts look better than the average font system, such as Arial or Times. Herein, I picked a font named Varela Round (`https://www.google.com/fonts/specimen/Varela+Round`).

4. Open `index.html`, and add the font style sheet within the `<head>` tag, as follows:

   ```
   <link rel='stylesheet' href='http://fonts.googleapis.com/
   css?family=Varela+Round' type='text/css'>
   ```

5. Now, we will change the `font-family` stack, which is currently specified as the Foundation default font, to use Varela Round.

6. To do so, open `_config.scss`, uncomment the variable named `$body-font-family`, and insert `"Varela Round"`, as follows:

```
$body-font-family: "Varela Round", "Helvetica Neue", "Helvetica", Helvetica, Arial, sans-serif;
```

Sass commenting

Typically, commenting will cause the code compiler or the engine to ignore the code—like a browser. However, it is also often used as an inline document, explaining what the code does.

Every programming language has its own way to comment on code. In CSS, it will be this way:

```
/* .property { content: "" }*/
```

In Sass, we can either use the CSS way, as shown previously, or add `//`, as follows:

```
// .property { content: "" }
```

When `//` is added at the beginning of the line, the compiler will completely ignore the line, and thus won't compile it.

7. We will style each of the website sections. To begin with, we will focus on the website header, and then, subsequently down to the footer. Let's start off by adding an image background. Open `_main.scss` and then add the following lines:

```
.startup-header {
  background: url('../img/banner.jpg') no-repeat center center fixed;
  background-size: cover;
}
```

CSS3 Background Size

Background size is a special CSS3 property that controls the background stretch. The value of the cover that we used in the preceding snippets will proportionally stretch the background image to entirely cover the container. Head to the following references for further assistance on the CSS3 Background Size:

- CSS Backgrounds and Borders Module Level 3 (http://www.w3.org/TR/css3-background/#the-background-size)

- *Perfect Full Page Background Image* by Chris Coyier (http://css-tricks.com/perfect-full-page-background-image/)

- Can I Use CSS3 Background Size? (http://caniuse.com/#feat=background-img-opts)

The image, however, is currently hidden at the back of the background color that applies to the top bar and a section in which Foundation named it Panel (`http://foundation.zurb.com/docs/components/panels.html`), as shown in the following screenshot:

8. Remove these background colors so that we can see through the background image. To do so, open the `_config.scss` file and uncomment the following lines:

```
$topbar-bg-color: #333;
$topbar-bg: $topbar-bg-color;
```

Change the value of the `$topbar-bg-color` variable from `#333` to `transparent`

```
$topbar-bg: transparent;
```

9. Uncomment this following line, which specifies the panel's background color:

```
$panel-bg: scale-color($white, $lightness: -5%);
```

Then, change the value to `transparent` as well:

```
$panel-bg: transparent;
```

Now, we can see the background image, which is shown in the following screenshot:

10. From the preceding screenshot, it is evident that the top bar and the panel background color have been removed, but some of the menu items still have it.

11. Let's remove these background colors. In `_config.scss`, uncomment the following line:

```
$topbar-dropdown-bg: #333;
```

And change the value to use the value of the `$topbar-bg` variable, as follows:

```
$topbar-dropdown-bg: $topbar-bg;
```

12. Save it and let a few seconds pass for the files to be compiled, and you should see now that the background color of those menu items are removed, as shown in the following screenshot:

13. Add `padding-top` to give more distance between the top bar and the upper boundary of the browser viewport:

```
.startup-header {
...
  .startup-top-bar {
    padding-top: rem-calc(30);
  }
}
```

And now, as you can see, there is more breadth therein:

The left-half of the image is before we add the padding-top,
and the right-half definitely is after we add the padding-top.

14. Give more padding at the top and bottom of the panel section; hence, we can view more of the background image. Nest the style rules under the `.startup-header`, as follows:

```
.startup-header {
  ...
  .startup-hero {
    padding-top: rem-calc(150px);
    padding-bottom: rem-calc(150px);
  }
}
```

15. Add the logo image, as follows:

```
.startup-name {
  max-width: 60px;
  a {
    text-indent: 100%;
    white-space: nowrap;
    overflow: hidden;
    background: url('../img/logo.svg') no-repeat center left;
    background-size: auto 90%;
    opacity: 0.9;
  }
}
```

Now we have the logo added, as follows:

16. Hover over the menu links in the top bar, and you will find it with a dark background color, as follows:

This background color is not quite right when it comes to the website's aesthetic as a whole, so let's remove that. In `_config.scss`, uncomment the following lines:

```
$topbar-link-bg-hover: #272727;
```

Then, change the value to transparent by inheriting the value of the `$topbar-bg` variable, as follows:

```
$topbar-link-bg-hover: $topbar-bg;
```

17. Turn the menu links to uppercase so that it looks slightly bigger. Set the variable named `$topbar-link-text-transform` in `_config.scss` from none to uppercase:

```
$topbar-link-text-transform: uppercase;
```

18. The next thing we will do is change the styles of the two buttons: `Login` and `Sign Up`. We will make it just a little bit more fashionable, and the following are all the new styles for these buttons; nest these lines under the `.startup-header`:

```
.startup-header {
...
.startup-top-bar {
  padding-top: rem-calc(30);
    ul {
$color: fade-out(#fff, 0.8);
$color-hover: fade-out(#fff, 0.5);
    background-color: transparent;
    .button {
@include transition (border 300ms ease-out, background-color 300ms
ease-out);
    }
    .log-in {
  padding-right: 0;
      > .button {
        background-color: transparent;
        border: 2px solid $color;
        color: #fff;
        &:hover {
        background-color: transparent;
        border: 2px solid $color-hover;
        color: #fff;
        }
      }
    }
    .sign-up {
      > .button {
        background-color: $color;
```

```
      border: 2px solid transparent;
      color: #fff;
      &:hover {
        background-color: $color-hover;
        border: 2px solid transparent;
      }
    }
   }
  }
 }
}
}
```

Now, the buttons should look as shown in the following screenshot. Hover over the button, and you will see nice little transition effects that we added through the `transition()` mixin of Bourbon:

However, it's worth noticing that I consider this merely as decoration. It's up to you to customize the button styles.

19. With buttons on a transparent background, let's make three menu link items on the left-hand side, namely, **PRICES**, **PRICING**, and **BLOG**, slightly transparent as well. To do so, uncomment and change the variable named `$topbar-link-color` in `_config.scss` to `fade-out(#fff, 0.3)`, as follows:

```
$topbar-link-color: fade-out(#fff, 0.3);
```

20. Then, let's give the links a transition effect. Add the following lines in `_main.scss`:

```
.startup-header {
...
  .startup-top-bar {
    ...
    a {
      @include transition(color 300ms ease-out);
    }
  }
}
```

21. Next, we will add a dark transparent layer on the header. By adding this dark layer, the text in the header can be more distinct over the background image.

Add the following lines in `_main.scss`:

```scss
.startup-header {
...
  .startup-top-bar,
  .startup-hero {
    background-color: fade-out(#000, 0.5);
  }
}
```

22. Add the following lines as our last touch for the header section:

```scss
.startup-header {
...
  .startup-hero {
    padding-top: rem-calc(150px);
    padding-bottom: rem-calc(150px);
    .hero-lead {
      color: darken(#fff, 30%);
    }
  }
...
}
```

Now, we have a nice header for the website, as you can see in the following screenshot:

23. With the website styled, we will move to the next section. Below the header, we have the feature section that contains a number of key features of our products and services. And these are all the styles for the feature section:

```
...
.startup-features {
  padding: rem-calc(90 0);
  figure {
    margin: 0;
  }
  .columns {
    margin-bottom: rem-calc(15);
  }
}
```

In the preceding snippet, we remove the margin from the figure element that wraps the image icon. This will give the image icons figure more room to span, as you can see in the following screenshot:

Easy

This web application is super easy to use. No complicated setup. It just works out of the box.

Easy

This web application is super easy to use. No complicated setup. It just works out of the box.

Secure

Your data is encrypted with the latest Kryptonian technology. It will never be shared to anyone. Rest assured, your data is totally safe.

Secure

Your data is encyrpted with the latest Kryptonian technology. It will never be shared to anyone. Rest assured, your data is totally safe.

Other than that, `margin-bottom`, as well as the padding we added in conjunction with it , simply gives this section more whitespace.

24. Below the feature section, we have the section that shows happy customers speaking. We call it the testimonial section. Add the following style rules to build on it:

```
.startup-testimonial {
  padding: rem-calc(90 0);
  text-align: center;
  background-color: darken(#fff, 2%);
  blockquote {
    font-size: rem-calc(24);
  }
```

```
figure {
  margin-top: 0;
  margin-bottom: 0;
  .avatar {
    border-radius: 50%;
    display: inline-block;
    width: 64px;
  }
}
figcaption {
  margin-top: rem-calc(20);
  color: darken(#fff, 30%);;
}
}
```

25. Also, remove the `blockquote` element's left-hand side border by changing the value of `$blockquote-border` in `_config.scss`, as follows:

```
$blockquote-border: 0 solid #ddd;
```

Note that the preceding styles are merely decoration. At this stage, this is how the testimonial section looks:

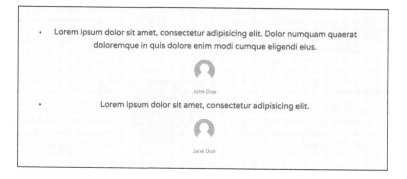

Don't freak out, it's not broken. The remaining styles will be added through the Orbit Slider plugin once it is enabled. We will take a look at the steps for this shortly.

26. Next, we will style the price and plan tables. These are all the styles for the table price, and their main purpose is to give each table a distinct color.

```
.startup-pricing {
  $basic-bg    : #85c1d0;
  $team-bg     : #9489a3;
```

```
$enterprise-bg : #d04040;

padding-top: rem-calc(120);
padding-bottom: rem-calc(120);
.pricing-table {
  background-color: darken(#fff, 2%);
}
.pricing-basic {
  .title {
    background-color: $basic-bg;
  }
  .price {
    background-color: lighten($basic-bg, 25%);
  }
}
.pricing-team {
  .title {
    background-color: $team-bg;
  }
  .price {
    background-color: lighten($team-bg, 25%);
  }
}
.pricing-enterprise {
.title {
    background-color: $enterprise-bg;
  }
  .price {
    background-color: lighten($enterprise-bg, 25%);
  }
  }
}
```

27. The footer section is bare and straightforward. There's nothing prominent. There is just a bunch of style rules to make the footer look nicer, as follows:

```
.startup-footer {
  $footer-bg: darken(#fff, 5%);
  text-align: center;
  padding: rem-calc(60 0 30);
  background-color: $footer-bg;
  border-top: 1px solid darken($footer-bg, 15%);
  .footer-nav {
    ul {
      margin-left: 0;
```

```
    }
    li {
      display: inline-block;
      margin: rem-calc(0 10);
    }
    a {
      color: darken($footer-bg, 30%);
      @include transition (color 300ms ease-out);
      &:hover {
        color: darken($footer-bg, 70%);
      }
    }
  }
  .social-nav {
    li a:before {
      margin-right: rem-calc(5);
      position: relative;
      top: 2px;
    }
    .foundicon-facebook:hover {
      color: #3b5998;
    }
    .foundicon-twitter:hover {
      color: #55acee;
    }
  }
  .footer-copyright {
    margin-top: rem-calc(30);
    color: darken($footer-bg, 15%);
  }
}
```

What just happened?

In this section, we focused on the website's appearance. We just added styles that eventually make the website look a lot nicer from the header and down to the footer. However, a few things are not workable at this stage, such as Orbit, and we have yet to test how the website looks in the smaller viewport size. So, that is exactly what we are going to address in the next section. This is how the website should now look at this stage:

Stay Cool and be Awesome

The most awesome web application in the galaxy.

Signup

Easy

This web application is super easy to use. No complicated setup. It just works out of the box.

Fast

This web application runs in a blink of eye. There is no other application that is on par with our application in term of speed.

Secure

Your data is encrypted with the latest Kryptonian technology. It will never be shared to anyone. Rest assured, your data is totally safe.

Awesome

It's simply the most awesome web application and make you the coolest person in the galaxy. Enough said.

- Lorem ipsum dolor sit amet, consectetur adipisicing elit. Dolor numquam quaerat doloremque in quis dolore enim modi cumque eligendi eius.

John Doe

- Lorem ipsum dolor sit amet, consectetur adipisicing elit.

Jane Doe

Basic	Team	Enterprise
$10/month	**$50**/month	**$300**/month
Perfect for personal use	For a small team.	For large corporation
1GB Storage	50GB Storage	Unlimited Storage
1 User	Up to 10 Users	Unlimited Users
24/7 Support	24/7 Support	24/7 Priority Support
Sign Up	Sign Up	Sign Up

About   Contact   Help   Careers   Terms   Privacy

Facebook   Twitter

Have a go hero – colors and creativities

I realize that good, bad, nice, and not nice are highly subjective. It all depends on individual preference and their degree of taste. So, if the website decoration, such as colors, fonts, and sizes, that we specified in the preceding steps are not up your alley, you can freely change them and add your own creativity.

Pop quiz – importing an external Sass style sheet

Q1. Hopefully, you followed the preceding steps fully through and paid attention to some of the minute details. We have imported a number of style sheets to compile them into a single style sheet. How do we make the Sass compiler ignore these imported style sheets so that the compiler won't compile them into a CSS file on its own?

1. Remove the extension file's extension in the import declaration.

2. Add an underscore as a prefix in the import declaration.

3. Add an underscore as a prefix in the file name.

Fine-tuning the website

As mentioned, there are a couple of things we need to do before we call the website done. First, we are going to enable Orbit and the toggle function of the top bar, and optimize the website styles, such as the positioning and the sizing, for smaller viewport size. It's time for action again.

Time for action – compiling JavaScript and styling the website with media queries

Perform the following steps to compile the JavaScript files and optimize the website for a small viewport size:

1. Create a new JavaScript file in the `assets/js` directory named `foundation.js`.

2. In `foundation.js`, import the following JavaScript files:

```
// @koala-prepend "../../components/foundation/js/vendor/jquery.js"
// @koala-prepend "../../components/foundation/js/foundation/
foundation.js"
// @koala-prepend "../../components/foundation/js/foundation/
foundation.topbar.js"
// @koala-prepend "../../components/foundation/js/foundation/
foundation.orbit.js"
```

3. Via Koala, compile `foundation.js`.

4. Then, open `index.html` and add the following lines right before `</body>` to enable the Orbit Slider functionalities:

```
<script src="assets/js/foundation.min.js"></script>
<script>
$(document).foundation({
    orbit: {
        timer_speed: 3000,
        pause_on_hover: true,
        resume_on_mouseout: true,
        slide_number: false
    }
});
</script>
```

5. Now, we will refine the website layout for smaller viewport viewing with media queries. To do so, we need to uncomment the variables that define the media query ranges used in Foundation, so that we can use them in our style sheets as well:

```
$small-range: (0em, 40em);
$medium-range: (40.063em, 64em);
$large-range: (64.063em, 90em);
$xlarge-range: (90.063em, 120em);
$xxlarge-range: (120.063em, 99999999em);


$screen: "only screen";

$landscape: "#{$screen} and (orientation: landscape)";
$portrait: "#{$screen} and (orientation: portrait)";

$small-up: $screen;
$small-only: "#{$screen} and (max-width: #{upper-bound($small-range)})";

$medium-up: "#{$screen} and (min-width:#{lower-bound($medium-range)})";
$medium-only: "#{$screen} and (min-width:#{lower-bound($medium-range)}) and (max-width:#{upper-bound($medium-range)})";

$large-up: "#{$screen} and (min-width:#{lower-bound($large-range)})";
```

```
$large-only: "#{$screen} and (min-width:#{lower-bound($large-
range)}) and (max-width:#{upper-bound($large-range)})";

$xlarge-up: "#{$screen} and (min-width:#{lower-bound($xlarge-
range)})";
$xlarge-only: "#{$screen} and (min-width:#{lower-bound($xlarge-
range)}) and (max-width:#{upper-bound($xlarge-range)})";

$xxlarge-up: "#{$screen} and (min-width:#{lower-bound($xxlarge-
range)})";
$xxlarge-only: "#{$screen} and (min-width:#{lower-bound($xxlarge-
range)}) and (max-width:#{upper-bound($xxlarge-range)})";
```

> We can utilize these variables within our own style sheets, as follows:
>
> ```
> @media #{$small-up} {
>
> }
> ```

6. Now, we will define a couple of style rules through these media queries to adjust the website's styles, particularly the sizing, positioning, and whitespace.

7. And these are all the style rules to add in `_responsive.scss`.

```
@media #{$small-up} {
  .startup-name a {
    position: relative;
    left: rem-calc(15);
  }
}
@media #{$small-only} {
  .startup-header {
    .startup-name a {
      background-size: auto 80%;
    }
    .startup-top-bar {
      padding-top: rem-calc(15);
      .top-bar-section {
        text-align: center;
      }
```

```scss
      .sign-up {
        padding-top: 0;
      }
    }
    .startup-hero {
      text-align: center;
    }
  }
  .startup-footer {
    .secondary-nav {
      li, a {
        display: block;
      }
      a {
        padding: rem-calc(10);
      }
    }
  }
}
@media #{$medium-up} {
  .startup-top-bar {
    .log-in {
      padding-right: 3px;
    }
    .sign-up {
      padding-left: 3px;
    }
  }
}
@media #{$large-only} {
    .startup-name a {
    position: relative;
    left: rem-calc(0);
  }
}
```

What just happened?

We just compiled the JavaScript to enable the Orbit Slider and the toggle function of the top bar. And we also refined the website layout for a smaller viewport size. And the following screenshot shows how the website looks in a small viewport:

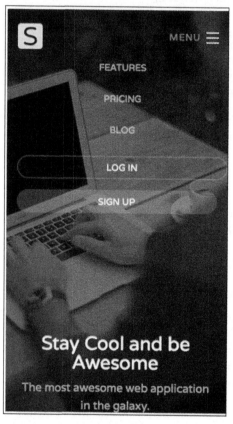

It is nice, isn't it?

Have a go hero – remove unnecessary Foundation components

We include all the Foundation components, even ones we are not using in the website. Hence, it is better to remove all the styles which do not give an advantage to the website. Open `_foundation.scss`, and comment the `@import` components that we do not need (at least at this moment) and recompile the style sheets.

Summary

We just finished working on the third project by building a responsive website for a new start-up company with Foundation. There are a lot of things we learned along the way to the end of this project, particularly about Sass. Sass is a powerful CSS preprocessor that allows us to compose styles in a more efficient and flexible form. We have learned to use variables, interpolation, mixins, and a couple of other Sass features.

Honestly speaking, the websites, including ones that we built in the previous chapters, are easy to build. Our work herein mostly involves making up the website appearance, such as the coloring and the sizing. Everything that matters most to make the website responsive, such as the Grid for example, has been covered by the frameworks we are using (Foundation, Bootstrap, and Responsive.gs).

To conclude, we hope the projects that we present in this book are a great start for you to build responsive websites on your own.

Pop Quiz Answers

Chapter 1, Responsive Web Design

Q1.	2
Q2.	2
Q3.	2

Chapter 2, Web Development Tools

Q1.	1
Q2.	2

Chapter 3, Constructing a Simple Respons3ive Blog with Responsive.gs

Pop quiz – using polyfill

Q1.	2

Pop quiz – HTML5 elements

Q1.	2
Q2.	2
Q3.	1

Chapter 4, Enhancing the Blog Appearance

Pop quiz – website performance rules

Q1.	4

Chapter 5, Developing a Portfolio Website with Bootstrap

Pop quiz – test your understanding on Bower commands

Q1.	2
Q2.	1
Q3.	2

Pop quiz – Bootstrap button classes

Q1.	5
Q2.	1

Chapter 6, Polishing the Responsive Portfolio Website with LESS

Pop quiz – which of the following option is not LESS Import option?

Q1.	5
Q2.	1

Pop quiz – using LESS function and extend syntax

Q1.	2
Q2.	1
Q3.	2

Chapter 8, Extend Foundation

Pop quiz – multiple parameters in Sass function

Q1.	3

Pop quiz – Sass color manipulation

Q1.	1

Pop quiz – importing external Sass style sheet

Q1.	1

Index

O

off-canvas navigation, Jasny Bootstrap
about 105-107
reveal menu, URL 107
slide-in menu, URL 107
Open Font Library
URL 77
Orbit
about 177
constructing 177, 178
URL 177, 178
OS X
Node.js, installing in 36, 37
XAMPP, installing in 28, 29

P

Pagination
URL 128
Panels
URL 128
parametric mixins
about 135, 136
default value, specifying 137
placeholder polyfill
URL 52
placeholder text styles
customizing 69
polyfills
Box sizing polyfills 48
used, for enhancing Internet Explorer 94, 95
used, for patching Internet Explorer 95, 96
portfolio website
layout, examining 108-110
polishing, with LESS 151
website styles, composing with
	LESS syntax 151-162
prefixes, Bootstrap responsive grid
col-lg- 100
col-md- 100
col-sm- 100
col-xs- 100
Prepros
URL 32
pricing tables 176

project dependencies
installing, with Bower 111-118
project dependency management, with Bower
about 35
command lines, references 38
Node.js, installing in OS X 36
Node.js, installing in Ubuntu 37
Node.js, installing in Windows 36
steps 37, 38
project directories
about 181
creating 51-55
organizing 51-55, 110-118, 181-183

R

referential import
about 141
variable, using in import statement 141
Rem
about 202, 203
URL 202
replace feature 133
Responsive embed
URL 128
responsive frameworks
about 12
Bootstrap framework 17
CSS preprocessors 18
features 13
Foundation framework 17
Responsive.gs
about 14, 42
CSS3 box sizing 15, 16
CSS box model 14, 15
polyfills 47
URL 52
responsive tables
URL 178
responsive web design
about 8
inspiration sources 21
reference recommendations 19, 20
URL 8
responsive websites, testing in browser
mobile emulator, using 34
source maps, using 33

Thank you for buying
Responsive Web Design by Example Beginner's Guide
Second Edition

About Packt Publishing

Packt, pronounced 'packed', published its first book "*Mastering phpMyAdmin for Effective MySQL Management*" in April 2004 and subsequently continued to specialize in publishing highly focused books on specific technologies and solutions.

Our books and publications share the experiences of your fellow IT professionals in adapting and customizing today's systems, applications, and frameworks. Our solution based books give you the knowledge and power to customize the software and technologies you're using to get the job done. Packt books are more specific and less general than the IT books you have seen in the past. Our unique business model allows us to bring you more focused information, giving you more of what you need to know, and less of what you don't.

Packt is a modern, yet unique publishing company, which focuses on producing quality, cutting-edge books for communities of developers, administrators, and newbies alike. For more information, please visit our website: www.packtpub.com.

About Packt Open Source

In 2010, Packt launched two new brands, Packt Open Source and Packt Enterprise, in order to continue its focus on specialization. This book is part of the Packt Open Source brand, home to books published on software built around Open Source licenses, and offering information to anybody from advanced developers to budding web designers. The Open Source brand also runs Packt's Open Source Royalty Scheme, by which Packt gives a royalty to each Open Source project about whose software a book is sold.

Writing for Packt

We welcome all inquiries from people who are interested in authoring. Book proposals should be sent to author@packtpub.com. If your book idea is still at an early stage and you would like to discuss it first before writing a formal book proposal, contact us; one of our commissioning editors will get in touch with you.

We're not just looking for published authors; if you have strong technical skills but no writing experience, our experienced editors can help you develop a writing career, or simply get some additional reward for your expertise.

[PACKT] open source ✤
PUBLISHING   community experience distilled

Magento Responsive Theme Design

ISBN: 9781783980369   Paperback: 110 pages

Leverage the power of Magento to successfully develop and deploy a responsive Magento theme

1. Build a mobile-, tablet-, and desktop-friendly e-commerce site.

2. Refine your Magento store's product and category pages for mobile.

3. Easy-to-follow, step-by-step guide on how to get up and running with Magento.

HTML5 and CSS3 Responsive Web Design Cookbook

ISBN: 9781849695442   Paperback: 204 pages

Learn the secrets of developing responsive websites capable of interfacing with today's mobile Internet devices

1. Learn the fundamental elements of writing responsive website code for all stages of the development lifecycle.

2. Create the ultimate code writer's resource using logical workflow layers.

3. Full of usable code for immediate use in your website projects.

4. Written in an easy-to-understand language giving knowledge without preaching.

Please check **www.PacktPub.com** for information on our titles

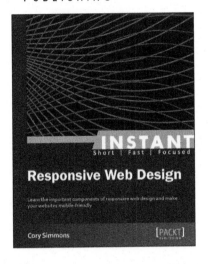

Instant Responsive Web Design

ISBN: 978-1-84969-925-9   Paperback: 70 pages

Learn the important components of responsive web design and make your websites mobile-friendly

1. Learn something new in an Instant! A short, fast, focused guide delivering immediate results.

2. Learn how to make your websites beautiful on any device.

3. Understand the differences between various responsive philosophies.

4. Expand your skill set with the quickly growing mobile-first approach.

Instant HTML5 Responsive Table Design How-to

ISBN: 978-1-84969-726-2   Paperback: 58 pages

Present your data anywhere on any device using responsive design techniques

1. Learn something new in an Instant! A short, fast, focused guide delivering immediate results.

2. Optimize and visualize your data using responsive design techniques.

3. Understand how responsive design works and which elements you should use to make your tables responsive.

4. Display numbers and filter data in small screens easily.

Please check **www.PacktPub.com** for information on our titles

Lightning Source UK Ltd.
Milton Keynes UK
UKOW07f1923010617
302500UK00017B/373/P